THE WORLD
ACCORDING TO GORE

THE WORLD ACCORDING TO GORE

The Incredible Vision of the Man Who Should Be President

Edited and with an Introduction
by Bill Katovsky

Skyhorse Publishing

www.skyhorsepublishing.com

Library of Congress Cataloging-in-Publication Data
Gore, Albert, 1948–
    The World According to Gore : The Incredible Vision of the Man
Who Should Be President / Edited and with an Introduction by
Bill Katovsky.
            p.   cm.
    Summary: A collection of quotes by former Vice President Al Gore.
    ISBN-13: 978-1-60239-232-8
    ISBN-10: 1-60239-232-3
    1. Gore, Albert, 1948–. Quotations.   2. Global warming—
Quotations, maxims, etc.   3. United States—Politics and
government—2001—Quotations, maxims, etc.   4. United States—
Politics and government—1993–2001—Quotations, maxims, etc.
    I. Katovsky, Bill.   II. Title.

E838.5.G672   2007
973.929092—dc22

                                                          2007029184

10   9   8   7   6   5   4   3   2   1

Printed in the United States of America

TABLE OF CONTENTS

Introduction ix

Climate in Crisis 1

The 2000 Presidential Race 61

Election Day 2000—The Aftermath 75

To Serve One's Country 87

Hollywood 103

Technology 109

The Media 129

The Accidental President: George W. Bush's
Reign of Lies, Terror, and Fear 141

Politics Today: Exposing a Flawed System 177

U.S. Foreign Policy 195

The Promise of America and the Challenge
of Democracy 205

Running for President Again 225

Miscellany 231

Notes and Acknowledgments 237

"If you entrust me with the presidency, I know I won't always be the most exciting politician. But I pledge to you tonight, I will work for you every day, and I will never let you down."
—Al Gore's acceptance speech at the Democratic National Convention, August 16, 2000

"Hi, I'm Al Gore and I used to be the next president of the United States of America."
—from *An Inconvenient Truth* (2006)

INTRODUCTION

This is no time for irony. Given that his personal crusade is halting global warming, former Vice President Al Gore is a man on fire.

He's burning up airwaves and electrifying packed auditoriums with his impassioned warning that our planet is teetering towards catastrophic meltdown. As co-organizer and impresario of Live Earth, the 24-hour, seven-continent concert series seen in 130 countries, Gore brought home this urgent message to millions of viewers. To help preach the secular gospel of a climate in crisis, he trained a small army of volunteers to present the slide show that formed the basis of *An Inconvenient Truth*.

His popularity among Democrats continues to trend upwards, almost like one of those temperature graphs in the Oscar-winning documentary. Some of this support comes from his scathing criticism of the Bush administration's chicanery and abuse of power.

From Madison to Manhattan, Gore followers wait for that day when he flicks on the campaign switch and says, "America, I'm in!" They include his pal, Steve Jobs of Apple, who told

Time, "We have dug ourselves into a 20-foot hole, and we need somebody who knows how to build a ladder. Al's the guy. Like many others, I have tried my best to convince him. So far, no luck."

The party faithful are waiting for Gore who will take back the White House from Republicans in 2008. A spirited group of netroots activists who have launched Web sites— DraftGore.com, AlGore.org, and RunAlGore.com—have attracted more than 100,000 online signatures.

As this book goes to press, Gore has repeatedly told interviewers that he's simply not interested in running again. But he won't entirely rule out the possibility that maybe, just maybe, he'll reconsider. "I am not thinking about being a candidate," he said to CNN's Larry King on May 22, 2007. "But, yes, it's true, I have not ruled it out for all time. I see no reason or necessity to do that." So the tiniest sliver of daylight remains for a late-in-the-game candidacy while Barack Obama, Hillary Clinton, and John Edwards distance themselves from the Democratic field.

Buoyed by the success of the film, which grossed over $50,000,000, and his recent bestseller, *The Assault on Reason,* which is a forceful indictment of America's political system undermined by an overreaching Executive Branch and apathetic public, Gore 2.0 is having way too much fun and making too much of an impact to give all that up and subject himself once more to the soul-crushing grind of the campaign trail.

Gore is the first to admit his own limitations as a crowd-pleasing vote-getter. "Most people in politics draw energy from backslapping and shaking hands and all that. I draw energy from discussing ideas," Gore told *New York* magazine. Need proof?

One of the biggest surprises about *An Inconvenient Truth* is his persuasive and genuinely captivating performance. He's the best science teacher you never had. Absent is the wooden Democratic nominee clumsily duking it out with his flat-footed Republican opponent in three 2000 presidential debates. The old, stiff Gore is stashed away in a lockbox. The new, limber Gore has been nominated for the Nobel Peace Prize.

There are other considerations keeping Gore out of the 2008 White House hunt. Most of his waking hours are devoted to sounding the alarm about climate change, which he insists "is the biggest challenge of our time." He's also involved in several successful business ventures that embody his lifelong fascination with technology and media. He co-founded youth-oriented cable network Current TV with former Democratic Party finance chairman Joel Hyatt. Predating YouTube in the creation of user-generated amateur content, Current TV reaches 46 million homes worldwide. In 2004, he teamed up with British money man David Blood to create an investment firm, Generation Investment Management, which funds companies in sustainable eco-friendly fields such as photovoltaic cells, wind turbines, wave energy, and solar power. Additionally, Gore sits on the board of directors at Apple and serves as a senior adviser to Google. Probably one of the smartest financial moves he ever made was joining Google in pre-IPO 2001 and receiving stock options now worth $30 million. And then there was Live Earth, which he tirelessly championed on behalf of its founder, British music promoter Kevin Wall. Gore even went backstage at the Grammy Awards and convinced the Red Hot Chili Peppers to perform at the star-studded ecopalooza.

In a recent interview with *The Tennessean*, Gore joked, "A couple of my friends have said over the last year, 'Al, why don't you take a break and run for president?'" With cover stories in *Wired, Entertainment Weekly,* and *Time,* Gore, 59, is having a breakthrough second career, happily basking in a newfound celebrity that must make his former political foes seethe with envy. Ozone Man is flying sky high.

Meanwhile, climate-change skeptics are retreating like melting glaciers. "The debate on global warming is over," declared *Scientific American* in a 2006 cover story. The planetary prophet had been correct all along regarding the danger of carbon-dioxide buildup in our atmosphere and oceans. Despite constant ridicule from naysayers as an owl-loving, tree-hugging alarmist, Gore always stayed true to his conviction that action is required to halt this frightening development. When he served in Congress and couldn't get his colleagues to pass legislation, he started giving his slide-show talk throughout the country. The creaky slide carousel got a tech makeover in 2001 when he digitalized the images and charts. He estimates that he's given the presentation at least a thousand times—in the U.S., Europe, and Asia. One city he missed was New Orleans. Gore told *Fast Company* that he had planned on being there the day Katrina hit. "The audience was the state insurance commissioners who wanted to learn more about hurricanes and global warming."

Environmental activist and Hollywood A-list player Laurie David encouraged Gore to turn his multimedia lecture into a documentary (she's the producer and Davis Guggenheim is the director), and as a consequence, Gore's message about climate change migrated far beyond the eco-fringe and reached the mainstream with surprising speed. A book based on *An*

Inconvenient Truth sold over 800,000 copies. Citizen Gore had awakened America, which emits one-quarter of the world's greenhouse gases. Grist.org, a heavily trafficked environmental Web site, nicknamed him Al Revere. Instead of redcoats, the new enemy is record temperatures in the red zone.

Throughout his twenty-four-year career in public office, first as a Congressman (he was only 28 when elected to the House), then as Senator (including a short-lived 1988 presidential run) and later as Bill Clinton's two-term vice president, the cerebral Gore was that rare breed of politician who could recite by chapter and verse complex policy issues—arms control, environment, government reform, technology—with the wonkish air of a think tank expert. His mind operates like a portable Wikipedia that's being continually updated with fresh facts and ideas. He relishes the role as public educator, and it's a pedagogical calling that he thought he could best achieve as U.S. president.

That 2000 election dealt a crushing, demoralizing blow to him, and to Democrats. Despite winning the popular vote, the Supreme Court narrowly sided (5-4) with George W. Bush's legal team concerning a Florida recount. It hurriedly handed a suspect victory to the Texas governor. The lesser man won. Gore nonetheless handled the defeat with steely grace and remarkable composure. During his televised concession speech on December 13, 2000, he said, "Let there be no doubt, while I strongly disagree with the court's decision, I accept it. I accept the finality of this outcome."

Asked to look back upon that tense, uncertain episode in America's electoral life nearly seven years later, Gore said this on *Charlie Rose:* "I've chosen not to challenge the rule of law because in our system there really is no intermediate step between a final Supreme Court decision and violent revolution."

Yet try to imagine his personal pain after Bush took the oath of office in January 2001. Somehow Gore managed to repress this enormous private hurt and found the inner strength to move on in life. Even among close friends, he refused to bare his soul regarding the gut-wrenching defeat. (To this day, the subject remains taboo.) He and wife Tipper vacated the capital and retreated to Nashville. He vanished from political life for months. *The Washington Post* noticed that he had become "the Greta Garbo of contemporary American politics." He taught classes at several universities. He co-authored two books about the American family with Tipper. They went on a summer sailing vacation in the Mediterranean. He grew a beard. They bought a 100-year-old home in an upscale neighborhood.

A speech at San Francisco's Commonwealth Club on September 21, 2002, marked Gore's return to the political arena. But it was a different, more outspoken man behind the lectern who voiced strong doubts about the White House's ill-considered decision to go after Saddam Hussein who had nothing to do with September 11. The media did an instant double take. They asked, "Who is this new Al and why didn't he talk like that during the last election?"

He continued giving speeches that criticized the Bush administration—its frontal assault on civil liberties, penchant for secrecy, institutionalized dishonesty, lack of accountability, endorsement of state-sanctioned torture, and the Iraq War. He astonished listeners with searing eloquence and astute insights. His confidence to let it rip and speak his mind grew with each talk Freed from the choke-chain grip of consultants and advisers, the liberated Gore could openly express his outrage over a broken political system hijacked by democracy-destroying zealots from the Republican party. With the exception of Fox News and its right-wing echo chamber, people now wanted to hear from the man whom many had written off as a political has-been.

His reemergence on the partisan battlefield, however, appeared tentative and awkward during the 2004 presidential primaries. Call it lousy timing or just more bad luck, because one month after he endorsed former Vermont governor Howard Dean came the Iowa scream. But this was a minor speed bump on Gore's road to career rehab. By the time he gave an address at the 2004 Democratic National Convention, a reinvigorated Gore stood tall as he cracked wise to the cheering crowd, "You win some, you lose some—and then there's that little-known third category."

It's impossible to avoid the fleeting indulgence of speculation. What if Florida had swung the other way and Gore became our forty-third president? The United States wouldn't be stuck in a military quagmire in Iraq, which Gore calls "the single worst strategic mistake in the history of this country." The Constitution wouldn't be force-fed into an Oval Office paper shredder. The judicial system wouldn't be stocked like a conservative trout farm. Dick Cheney wouldn't be running his own shadow government. Abu Ghraib and Guantanamo wouldn't be permanent stains on our country's conscience. No illegal domestic spying. No huge tax cuts benefiting the super wealthy. Instead of a gargantuan budget deficit, there'd probably still be a surplus. Our public lands wouldn't be held hostage to oil, gas, mining, and timber interests. The nation would be greener, cleaner, healthier, safer and more optimistic about its future.

The White House deception that pushed the country into war with Iraq, says Gore, is similar to the disinformation campaign that has undermined the scientific community's long-standing warning about a hotter planet. "In both cases the policies are badly mistaken," he stated on *CNN Larry King Live,* "and in both cases the evidence is available, overwhelming evidence to convince any reasonable person ahead of time that we should have done the opposite of what we did." With Iraq, fiction about WMD was disseminated as fact through propaganda and fear. A submissive media went along with the White House's unsubstantiated claim that "we don't want the next smoking gun to be a mushroom cloud." But with climate change, the information flow was reversed. To spread doubt and curtail debate, scientific facts were dismissed as hooey by the Bush administration and its big business supporters. Political considerations took precedence over hard science.

If anything, Gore is an extremely rational person. He knows what it will take to move millions of minds to accept the looming specter of global warming. Because attitudes and lifestyle habits are resistant to change, he's dedicated himself full-throttle to altering public opinion about climate change. There's a touching, almost poignant scene towards the end of *An Inconvenient Truth* when Gore quietly says, "The only way I know to do it is city by city, person by person, family by family." Fortunately, the climate's Cassandra now has help. The non-profit and non-partisan Alliance for Climate Protection—Gore is its chairman—plans to educate the public through widespread media exposure and grassroots education. Proceeds from the book, movie, and Live Earth event went to the Alliance. Current TV will air specially made commercials and promotions. Synergy indeed rocks Gore's world.

Since Gore likes speaking in metaphors, let's use one here to describe his mission: he's a twenty-first century Atlas holding aloft the sky on his broad shoulders. He threw down the global-warming gauntlet during his acceptance speech at the 2007 Academy Awards: "My fellow Americans, people all over the world, we need to solve the climate crisis. It's not a political issue, it's a moral issue." To simply do nothing will create a cascading effect of irreversible harm: longer heat waves, massive ice shelves splintering off Greenland and Antarctica, rising sea levels, coastal flooding, increased malaria, stronger hurricanes and monsoons, and poverty-inducing drought that will sweep barren wide swaths of Africa. It's goodbye planet and hello apocalypse.

This book opens a window to Al Gore—his thinking, his motivations, his beliefs, his politics, his passions. This compilation contains excerpts from his speeches, debates, interviews, and books. Here is Al Gore in his own words—erudite, visionary, analytical, heartfelt, and witty. Though the starting point is climate crisis, you will find quotes and passages covering a broad range of topics: Iraq War, the Bush White House, media, technology, the 2000 presidential election, the current state of politics, and the future and challenge of democracy in America.

BILL KATOVSKY
Northern California
August 2007

CLIMATE IN CRISIS

"Antarctica is the frontier of the ecological crisis. [It] plays a far more significant role than any other part of the Earth in the global climate system. For one thing, the cold waters surrounding the continent absorb more carbon dioxide from the atmosphere than all the rain forests. Antarctica is the single most powerful engine driving the world's weather, redistributing its massive coldness through the winds of the air and the currents of the sea. As greenhouse gases trap more heat in the Earth's atmosphere and temperatures climbs, they are expected to climb fastest of all here in Antarctica."

—Al Gore's "Unbearable Whiteness,"
The New Republic, December 2, 1988

"Nuclear war is an apocalyptic subject, and so is global environmental destruction. [We must sound the alarm] loudly and clearly of imminent and grave danger."

—speech at The National Academy of Sciences, as quoted in the *Memphis Commercial Appeal,* August 5, 1990

"I've been trying to tell this story for a long time, and I feel as if I have failed to get the message across."
—from opening sequence of *An Inconvenient Truth*

"Many scientists are now uncharacteristically scared. For the first time, we can see in the numbers that the rate of increase in global warming is accelerating."
—*Rolling Stone,* June 12-28, 2007

"I feel like the country singer who spends 30 years on the road to become an overnight sensation. And I've seen public interest [on global warming] wax and wane before—but this time does feel different."
—*Time,* May 16, 2007

"The planet has a fever. If your baby has a fever, you go to the doctor. If the doctor says you need to intervene here, you don't say, 'Well, I read a science fiction novel that told me it's not a problem.' If the crib's on fire, you don't speculate that the baby is flame retardant. You take action."
—testimony before the U.S. House of Representatives Subcommittee on Energy & Environment, March 21, 2007

"Our home—Earth—is in danger. What is at risk of being destroyed is not the planet itself, but the conditions that have made it hospitable for human beings. Without realizing the consequences of our actions, we have begun to put so much carbon dioxide into the thin shell of air surrounding our world that we have literally changed the heat balance between Earth and the Sun. If we don't stop doing this pretty quickly, the average temperature will increase to levels humans have never known and put an end to the favorable climate balance on which our civilization depends."

—Al Gore's op-ed "Moving Beyond Kyoto,"
New York Times, July 1, 2007

"This is not a political issue. This is a moral issue. It affects the survival of human civilization. It is not a question of left vs. right; it is a question of right vs. wrong. Put simply, it is wrong to destroy the habitability of our planet and ruin the prospects of every generation that follows ours."

—speech at New York University School of Law,
September 18, 2006

"We are facing a global climate crisis. It is deepening. We are entering a period of consequences."

"You look at that river gently flowing by. You notice the leaves rustling with the wind. You hear the birds."

—from *An Inconvenient Truth*

"Kevin Wall, the executive producer of these Live Earth concerts, saw [*An Inconvenient Truth*] and he and his wife were moved by it and he contacted me and mutual friends introduced us and we got to know each other really well. He is the only one who can pull off these Live Earth concerts on all seven continents. I've had the opportunity to contact a lot of the greatest performers in the world and ask them if they would do this and—and they all are doing it—150 of the very best performers in the entire world. All of the performers, by the way, are performing for free. It's the launch of a three-year campaign to get the message about the climate crisis and the solutions to the climate crisis to every person on earth so that we can move across this political tipping point, beyond which everybody in every country puts pressure on their leaders and every party to make this a top priority and solve the climate crisis."

—*CNN Larry King Live,* July 5, 2007

"A new study says that the North Polar icecap is now melting three times faster than the most pessimistic projections were just a few years ago and could be completely gone in as little as 35 years, but we can still save it if we act quickly. And that's what the Live Earth concerts are all about, that to get past the naysayers and the cynics and the carbon polluters and instead lay the truth before the people of this country and the world and define it properly as a moral issue."

—*CNN Larry King Live,* July 5, 2007

"As more and more people understand what's at stake, they become a part of the solution, and share both in the challenges and opportunities presented by the climate crises."

"Even though the earth is of such vast size, the most vulnerable part of the global environment is the atmosphere—because it is surprisingly thin—as the late Carl Sagan used to say: like a coat of varnish on a globe."

—from *An Inconvenient Truth*

"The Earth has two lungs—the forests and the southern ocean. Unfortunately, we are destroying our forests at the rate of one football field every second, an area the size of Tennessee every year. Since the oceans of the world contain 50 times as much carbon dioxide as the atmosphere, even small changes in the temperature-sensitive mechanism by which carbon dioxide is transferred back and forth between the oceans can have profound implications."

—Al Gore's "Unbearable Whiteness,"
The New Republic, December 2, 1988

"When I was an undergraduate I was privileged to sign up for a course offered by the first person to measure CO_2 in the earth's atmosphere. He was a visionary, and he saw that the postwar economic boom powered by coal and oil was beginning to radically change the concentration of CO_2 in the atmosphere—and he knew atmospheric chemistry, and he knew what it would do to outgoing infrared radiation. So he started this historic set of measurements out in the middle of the Pacific. He shared his measurements with my undergraduate class, and he explained what it meant and sketched the future implications in such a compelling way that it was different from other experiences I had in college. I kept in touch with him, and later when I was elected to Congress—10 years later, or less—I helped organize the first hearings on this issue and had him as the lead-off witness."

—*Newsweek*, April 28, 2006

"In our time, the CO_2 graph is just going right through the roof. For 400,000 years, as far back as we can measure, these CO_2 and temperature levels have gone up and down in lock-step, and now we're pushing the world over the brink of a new reality—CO_2 levels not seen in tens of millions of years. The magnitude of changes now in prospect are far larger on the warm side than the changes on the cold side that produced ice ages. The increasing frequency of violent weather events is in keeping with the volatility that scientists have told us to anticipate with global warming. Stronger storms, melting ice, rising sea levels."

—*Outside,* August 2000

"*Scientific American* introduces the lead article in its special issue this month with the following sentence: 'The debate on global warming is over.'"

—speech at New York University School of Law, New York City, September 18, 2006

"Even junkies find veins in their toes."

—referring to the excess energy used to extract oil from western Canada's tar sands

"The planet is in distress and all of the attention is on Paris Hilton. We have to ask ourselves what is going on here?"
—*The Sun* (UK), June 18, 2007

"If we put our minds to it, think about this: before we spend vast hundreds of billions of dollars on an unimaginative and retread effort to make a tiny portion of the moon habitable for a handful of people, we ought to focus instead on a massive effort to ensure that planet earth is habitable for future generations of people right here."
—speech to MoveOn.org, New York City, January 14, 2004

"I remember one part of my own journey a decade ago. The trip was on the *U.S.S. Pargo*—a nuclear submarine that traveled under the Arctic ice sheet all the way from Greenland to the North Pole. When we reached the pole, the sub broke through the summer icepack—and as I climbed through the hatch, I caught my first glimpse of the North Pole. The light was stunningly bright; clouds of ice crystals sparkled in the frozen air. That submarine was part of a U.S. fleet patrolling secret routes under the ice—routes that took our subs and missiles close to the former Soviet Union's northern border. In the process, the Navy had been collecting data about the thickness of the ice cap—merely to identify spots where subs could break through the ice. Most of the information that was gathered had no national security purpose—so it was recorded and stored, but never examined or analyzed. It was 'exformation'—it existed, but no one knew what it said. As that submarine returned from the pole, deep beneath the ice, it occurred to me that if we shared this data with scientists, we could map a timeline of the ice cap, and the effects of global warming.

When I returned to Washington, I began to discuss the idea with our military and intelligence agencies. One hundred top environmental scientists gained top-secret clearance to review the data, and scrub it of anything that could compromise our national security. Later, as Vice President, I held a conference with Russian government officials and scientists, where both sides agreed to share our scrubbed data about the Arctic—as well as previously-secret sonar and satellite data about the northern ocean. The results were startling. We learned that the Arctic ice cap had thinned by 40 percent since the 1970s—a story that made headlines all over the world. The loss has averaged four inches a year for the past decade."

—speech on Earth Day 2000

"Since we gathered at the Rio Conference in 1992, both scientific consensus and political will have come a long way. We have reached a fundamentally new stage in the development of human civilization, in which it is necessary to take responsibility for a recent but profound alteration in the relationship between our species and our planet. Because of our new technological power and our growing numbers, we now must pay careful attention to the consequences of what we are doing to the Earth—especially to the atmosphere."

—speech at Kyoto Climate Change Conference,
Kyoto, Japan, December 8, 1997

"The most vulnerable part of the Earth's environment is the very thin layer of air clinging near to the surface of the planet that we are now so carelessly filling with gaseous wastes that we are actually altering the relationship between the Earth and the Sun—by trapping more solar radiation under this growing blanket of pollution that envelops the entire world. The extra heat which cannot escape is beginning to change the global patterns of climate to which we are accustomed, and to which we have adapted over the last 10,000 years. Each of the 160 nations here has brought unique perspectives to the table, but we all understand that our work in Kyoto is only a beginning. None of the proposals being debated here will solve the problem completely by itself. But if we get off to the right start here, we can quickly build momentum as we learn together how to meet this challenge. Our first step should be to set realistic and achievable, binding emissions limits, which will create new markets for new technologies."

—speech at Kyoto Climate Change Conference,
Kyoto, Japan, December 8, 1997

Q: Why wasn't the Kyoto Protocol ratified during the Clinton-Gore years?
A: When I returned from Kyoto, I could only convince one out of all 100 senators to commit to ratifying it. Paul Wellstone was the only one. I was in favor of pushing the process in spite of that, but I couldn't quarrel with the good sense of President Clinton in saying, 'Well, look, if there's no more support than

that, then this is a quixotic task.' That experience was part of what caused me to embark on this effort to change the minds of the American people.

—*Sierra,* September/October 2006

"If I had been president, would I have bent every part of the administration and every part of the White House to support [the Kyoto pact]? Yes, I would have."

—*New York Times,* May 20, 2007

"I am proud of my role during the Clinton administration in negotiating the Kyoto protocol. But I believe that the protocol has been so demonized in the United States that it probably cannot be ratified here."

—Al Gore's op-ed "Moving Beyond Kyoto,"
New York Times, July 1, 2007

"[Critics have] lost the argument and they don't want to stop dumping all this pollution into the Earth's atmosphere. The only thing they have left is cash and now they're offering cash for so-called skeptics who will try to confuse people about what the science really say. But it's unethical because now the time has come when we have to act."

—*Cuatro* (Spanish television), February, 6, 2007

"The melting of the North Pole is one of the most urgent catastrophes that should be prevented as quickly as we can convince people to act. It's a fairly thin floating ice cap, and as you know, the Arctic and the Antarctic are very different. The Arctic is ocean surrounded by land while the Antarctic is land surrounded by ocean, and that makes all the difference in the thickness of the ice. It's 10,000 feet thick in the Antarctic and less than 10 feet thick in the Arctic. Much less now. The North Polar ice cap is in grave danger now. And nearby the great ice mound of Greenland is under increasing pressure from growing temperatures also. If that were to melt, or to break up and slip into the sea, it would raise sea level 20 feet worldwide."

—*Fresh Air with Terry Gross*, NPR, May 30, 2006

"Earlier this year, yet another team of scientists reported that the previous twelve months saw 32 glacial earthquakes on Greenland between 4.6 and 5.1 on the Richter scale—a disturbing sign that a massive destabilization may now be underway deep within the second largest accumulation of ice on the planet."

—speech at New York University School of Law, New York City, September 18, 2006

"If Greenland were to break up and slip into the sea or West Antarctica, or half of either and half of both, it would be a 20-feet increase, and that would lead to more than 450 million climate refugees. The direct impacts on the U.S. have already begun. Today, 49 percent of America is in conditions of drought or near drought. We have fires in California, in Florida, in other states, directly correlated with higher temperatures, which dry out the soils, dry out the vegetation. We have a very serious threat of losing enough soil moisture in a hotter world that agriculture here in the United States would be greatly affected."

—*CNN Larry King Live*, May 22, 2007

"Scientists studying Emperor penguins at the colony featured in [*March of the Penguins*] found that their numbers have dropped by 70% since the 1960s. The likely culprit: global climate change. Warmer temperatures and stronger winds produce thinner sea ice, the frozen ocean water on which the penguins nest. The weakened ice is more likely to break apart and drift out to sea, taking the penguins' eggs and chicks with it."

—from *An Inconvenient Truth* (book)

"I've seen times in the past when there was a flurry of concern about global warming, and then, like a summer storm, it faded. But this time, it may be different."

—*Sierra,* September/October 2006

"Noah was commanded to preserve biodiversity."

—*New York* magazine, May 22, 2006

"I [gave] a full presentation of the slide show in the Great Hall of the People in China when I was vice president. A lot of the speeches and events and messages on global warming were not seen as being on the 'A' list of issues to be covered by the news media. So a lot of what I tried to do to get more attention to it seemed as if it didn't take place because it didn't make it through that filter."

—*Newsweek,* April 28, 2006

"China and the United States are the two biggest sources of global warming pollution. And, of course, the Chinese standard of living is so much lower than ours for the average person. They have a right to aspire to a higher quality of life. But they shouldn't have to repeat the mistakes that we made 100 years ago and continue burning so much dirty fuel, without capturing the carbon pollution and keeping it from going into the atmosphere. So, it's very significant, by the way, that the Chinese authorities are allowing [the Live Earth] concert in Shanghai. It's going to be broadcast all over China."

—*CNN Larry King Live,* July 5, 2007

"[My] friend, Dr. Lonnie Thompson of Ohio State University, is the world's leading expert on mountain glaciers. He predicts that within 10 years there will be no more 'snows of Kilimanjaro.'"

—from *An Inconvenient Truth* (book)

"Everywhere I go, I find rising awareness, a growing sense of urgency and a building determination and commitment to solve the climate crisis. I am very optimistic that we are getting closer and closer to the political tipping point that is necessary to embolden the political leaders in every party to make the policy changes that are so necessary."

—from AlGore.com blog entry, April 5, 2007

"After I left the White House in January 2001, I once again started giving a slide show on global warming on a regular basis. The first time I took the slides out of storage and held them up to the light and combined them into one carousel, went down to Middle Tennessee State University to give my slide show, and they were all backward. It was a very awkward and embarrassing moment, and I went back home to Nashville and Tipper said, 'I knew I should have put those in for you.' And then she said, 'By the way, Mr. Information Super Highway, we have computers now and you should put them on your computer.' And at that point, I started to give it a lot more frequently—several times a week. At one of the showings in Los Angeles several people from the entertainment industry came up afterward and talked to me, and said, 'Would you consider making this into a movie?'"

—*Newsweek*, April 28, 2006

"I've trained 1200 people to go out and give my [global warming] slide show multiple times every day, all over this country. They're a great group of people—completely bipartisan, by the way, from all walks of life. And I'm continuing to give it myself."

—*The New Republic* online, June 13, 2007

"Trust me on this. If audiences had an unlimited attention span, I'd be in my second term as President. You're telling some not only inconvenient truths but hard truths, and it can be scary as hell. You're not going to get people to go with you if you paralyze them with fear."

—speaking to slide-show lecture trainees
in Nashville, Tennessee, *Time,* May 16, 2007

"I update the slide show every time I give it. I add new images because I learn more about it every time I give it. It's like beachcombing, Every time the tide comes in and out you find some more shells."

—speech at TED Talks, Monterey, CA, June 27, 2006

"I'm going to be launching a training program in China to train lots of Chinese people to give my slide show, in Chinese, all across China."

—CNN *Larry King Live,* July 5, 2007

"I have probably given this slide show a thousand times. The thing I have spent more time on than anything else in the slide show is trying to identify all those things in people's minds that serve as obstacles to them understanding this. Whenever I feel that I have identified an obstacle, I try to take it apart, roll it around, move it, demolish it, blow it up. I set myself a goal to communicate this real clearly. The only way I know to do it is city by city, person by person, family by family. I have faith that pretty soon enough minds will have changed that we cross a threshold."

—from *An Inconvenient Truth*

"Global warming is complex, and there's not a single magic answer to global warming, but developing a clear understanding of what the challenge is, and then mobilizing people to become part of the common effort to solve it, that's the answer. There's an African proverb that says, 'If you want to go quickly, go alone. If you want to go far, go together.' We have to go far, quickly."

—*Charlie Rose*, May 25, 2007

"I have enjoyed the luxury of being able to focus single-mindedly on this issue. But I am under no illusions that any position has as much ability to influence change as the presidency does. If the President made climate change the organizing principle, the filter through which everything else had to flow, then that could really make a huge difference."

—*Time*, May 16, 2007

"Category 5 denial is an enormous obstacle to any discussion of solutions. Nobody is interested in solutions if they don't think there's a problem."

—Grist.org, May 9, 2006

"The global environmental crisis is, as we say in Tennessee, real as rain, and I cannot stand the thought of leaving my children with a degraded earth and diminished future. That's the basic reason why I have searched so intensively for ways to understand this crisis and help solve it."

—from Al Gore's *Earth in the Balance*

"H. G. Wells wrote that 'history is a race between education and catastrophe.' And this is potentially the worst catastrophe in the history of civilization. The challenge now is to seize our potential for solving this crisis without going through a cataclysmic tragedy that would be the climate equivalent of wartime attack. And it's particularly important because, by the nature of this crisis, when the worst consequences begin to manifest themselves, it will already be too late."

—*Sierra,* September/October 2006

"When I first wrote *Earth in the Balance* [in 1992], I could not have predicted the political upheavals to come. Nor could I have predicted how long it would take for the scientific consensus to solidify. The nature and severity of the climate crisis had seemed painfully obvious to me for quite a long time; but in retrospect, I wish that we could have had in the 1990s the deafening scientific consensus that has emerged in more recent years. It would have been much easier to galvanize the public and persuade the Congress to act."

—from Al Gore's foreword to *Earth in the Balance* (2006)

"Consider this tale of two planets. Earth and Venus are almost exactly the same size, and have almost exactly the same amount of carbon. The difference is that most of the carbon on Earth is in the ground—having been deposited there by various forms of life over the last 600 million years—and most of the carbon on Venus is in the atmosphere. As a result, while the average temperature on Earth is a pleasant 59 degrees, the average temperature on Venus is 867 degrees. True, Venus is closer to the Sun than we are, but the fault is not in our star; Venus is three times hotter on average than Mercury, which is right next to the Sun. It's the carbon dioxide."

—Al Gore's op-ed "Moving Beyond Kyoto,"
New York Times, July 1, 2007

Q: How do you feel about Senator Inhofe, who has been, I guess, the most strong critic of yours in the Senate, who calls climate change "a hoax"?

A: Well, you know, there's some people who still think that the earth is flat. I just don't know what to say to them.

—CNN *Larry King Live,* July 5, 2007

"Do you realize the leading scientists in the world now say that if the current rate of species loss continues, more than half of all the living creatures God put on this earth will disappear within the lifetimes of our children. Extinction is a natural process, but now it's proceeding a thousand times faster than it has ever happened in the last sixty-five million years, because of what our civilization is doing. And we've got to speak out and stop that."

—*Booknotes*, February 16, 1992

"*Silent Spring* planted the seeds of a new activism that has grown into one of the great popular forces of all time. When Rachel Carson died, in the spring of 1964, it was becoming clear that her voice would never be silenced. She had awakened not only our nation but the world. The publication of *Silent Spring* can properly be seen as the beginning of the modern environmental movement. For me personally, *Silent Spring* had a profound impact. It was one of the books we read at home at my mother's insistence and then discussed around the dinner table. Indeed, Rachel Carson was one of the reasons I became so conscious of the environment and so involved with environmental issues."

—from Al Gore's introduction to
a new edition of *Silent Spring*, 1994

"The discussion of positive feedback loops has become quite common with scientists concerned with environmental crisis. Halting the burning of forests is an important strategy for reducing the rate of CO_2 increase, and massive tree planting programs represent a good way to pull carbon out of the atmosphere."

—from Al Gore's *Earth in the Balance*

"If we are here for any purpose whatsoever, it certainly is not to destroy the only home we have."

—speech at the University of Redlands, Redlands, California, November 7, 2006

"The complexity [of global warming] by itself is an obstacle [to get the message across to politicians]. There's a natural tendency to avoid thinking about the subjects that might involve some psychic pain, and the idea that human civilization is colliding with the earth's environment is a painful reality. Nothing in our history or culture prepares us for the new reality, the new relationship between human civilization and the planet's ecosystem. We've quadrupled our population globally in the last hundred years, and we've magnified the power of our technologies thousands of times over. And when you combine those two elements, 6.5 billion people times incredibly powerful ways of exploiting nature, and then you mix in a new philosophy of discounting the future consequences of present actions, it produces this new collision, the most dangerous part of which is global warming."

—*Fresh Air with Terry Gross*, NPR, May 30, 2006

"Another reason that it has been difficult to communicate the truth [about global warming], the inconvenient truth if you will, about this planetary emergency, and that is that some interests—political, business and ideological that strongly resist the truth here—have used every means at their disposal to confuse people, to put out misinformation. And really the consensus on global warming is as strong as it gets in science, and the naysayers are so isolated and so without any support or respect in the mainstream science community. It is partly the oil company disinformation campaign that keeps their message out there."

—*Fresh Air with Terry Gross*, NPR, May 30, 2006

"The largest polluters close their ears and spend millions of dollars a year trying to intentionally confuse people into thinking [global warming] isn't real, the same way that tobacco companies spent millions of dollars to try to convince people that the doctors weren't really saying that smoking causes lung disease. And that was really unethical what they did. And what these polluters are doing now is also unethical."

—*CNN Larry King Live,* July 5, 2007

"I believe it is appropriate to have an over-representation of factual presentations on how dangerous [global warming] is, as a predicate for opening up the audience to listen to what the solutions are, and how hopeful it is that we are going to solve this crisis."

—Grist.org, May 9, 2006

"Misconception #8: 'The warming scientists are recording is just the effect of cities trapping heat, rather than anything to do with greenhouse gases.' People who want to deny global warming because it's easier than dealing with it try to argue that what scientists are really observing is just the 'urban heat island' effect, meaning that cities tend to trap the heat because of all the buildings and asphalt. This is simply wrong. Most scientific research shows that 'urban heat islands' have a negligible effect on the overall warming of the planet."

—from *An Inconvenient Truth* (book)

"I was scheduled to give the slide show in New Orleans that day [Katrina hit]. The audience was the state insurance commissioners who wanted to learn more about hurricanes and global warming."

—*Fast Company*, July 2007

"Global warming may not affect the frequency of hurricanes, but it makes the average hurricane stronger, magnifying its destructive power. In the years ahead, there will be more storms like Katrina. Hurricanes are heat engines that thrive on warm water. We know that heat-trapping gases from our industrial society are warming the oceans. We know that, in the past thirty years, the number of Category 4 and 5 hurricanes globally has almost doubled. It's time to connect the dots."

—Al Gore, "The Time to Act is Now,"
Rolling Stone, November 3, 2005

"Katrina was a tipping point for millions of Americans. A top insurance executive at Lloyd's of London said just the other week that if we don't act now to prevent this looming catastrophe, 'we will face extinction.' You know—just a typical, long-haired hippie at Lloyd's of London."

—*Rolling Stone,* July 13–27, 2006

"The [Hurricane Katrina] refugees that we have seen—I don't like that word when applied to American citizens in our own country—but the refugees that we have seen could well be the first sip of that bitter cup because sea-level rise in countries around the world will mobilize millions of environmental refugees."

—speech to the Sierra Summit, San Francisco,
September 9, 2005

"I was skeptical about the movie at first. I couldn't understand what these Hollywood producers were thinking. I didn't see how the slide show could be a movie. But, you know, they were right. Almost two million people have seen *An Inconvenient Truth* in theaters. That's two million people whose minds may be changed by the film. That's not something you can do with a slide show."

—*Entertainment Weekly,* July 21, 2006

"The slide show is a living, breathing thing. I have a slide show genome that's five times larger than the slide show I actually give. And depending on the audience—if the audience is made up of people who are still in [profound] denial, then it's way heavy on the evidence of the reality of [global warming]. If it's an audience that already knows all that and they want to talk much more about how we can get moving more quickly on solutions, then it's heavy on that. But for the country as a whole, America's still in a bubble of unreality. Along with Australia, it's one of only two nations on Earth in the advanced nation category that has not ratified Kyoto and doesn't accept the reality of this crisis."

—*The Stranger* (Seattle), June 1, 2006

Q: You advertise the movie as "by far the most terrifying film you will ever see." For Europeans the most terrifying aspect is how little most Americans seem to know about global warming. How do you explain that?

A: The purpose of the movie and the book is to change that. But as to why that's the case: The oil companies and the coal companies have too much influence in the U.S. Bush and Cheney have led us in the wrong direction. But it's also true that a lot of Democrats are resistant to change on this issue. I think it has to do with our political history and culture, with our "frontier mentality," which used to mean striking out for new horizons and now I think plays into our habit of driving great distances.

—*Der Spiegel* (Germany), July 21, 2006

"The relationship between our civilization and the earth has been radically transformed."

"As it happens, some of the most disturbing images of environmental destruction can be found exactly halfway between the North and South pole—precisely at the equator in Brazil—where billowing clouds of smoke regularly blacken the sky above the immense but now threatened Amazon rain forest. Acre by acre, the rain forest is being burned to create fast pasture for fast-food beef. There are more different species of birds in each square mile of the Amazon than exist in all of North America—which means we are silencing thousands of songs we have never even heard."

—from Al Gore's *Earth in the Balance*

"I've always heard that when the ground starts spitting coffins back up, it's not a good sign."

—speech at the University of Redlands, Redlands, California, November 7, 2006

"The central challenge is to expand the limits of what's now considered politically possible. The outer boundary of what's considered plausible today still falls far short of the near boundary of what would actually solve the crisis."

—*New York Times*, May 20, 2007

"The serious debate over the climate crisis has now moved on to the question of how we can craft emergency solutions in order to avoid this catastrophic damage. This debate over solutions has been slow to start in earnest not only because some of our leaders still find it more convenient to deny the reality of the crisis, but also because the hard truth for the rest of us is that the maximum that seems politically feasible still falls far short of the minimum that would be effective in solving the crisis."

—speech at New York University School of Law, New York City, September 18, 2006

"We live in a civilization that has developed rather fully according to a pattern that emphasizes the burning of carbon-based fuels. So making the shift to renewable energy is a challenge for everyone that will be a lot easier when governments around the world adopt the new strategies that will make this shift a lot easier to accomplish."

—*The Sun* (UK), June 18, 2007

"Our global civilization is now at the equivalent of a ten-pack-a-day habit. You know all those oil wells that were on fire in Kuwait, with the smoke blackening the sky? All of them put together on the worst day put less than one percent of the pollution into the earth's atmosphere that we put into the earth's atmosphere every day. And some people who are addicted to alcohol, for example, will see a string of drunk-driving accidents as unrelated misfortunes, when actually, they're connected. Well, we look around the world now and we see these ecological catastrophes that are beginning to resume what the comedian A. Whitney Brown called a 'nature hike through the book of Revelation,' and yet a lot of people see them as just sort of unconnected misfortunes and wonder, 'Well, what's going on?'"

—*Booknotes,* February 16, 1992

"I have come here today because Glacier National Park faces a grave threat to its heritage—and it's one that can't be met with a simple local restoration plan. The fifty glaciers in this park—which date back to the last Ice Age, 10,000 years ago—are melting away at an alarming rate. Over the last century, we have lost nearly three-quarters of all the glaciers in this park. If this trend continues, in about thirty years, there won't be any glaciers left at all. To borrow a phrase from a well-know pop musician, this could become the Park Formerly Known as Glacier. What's happening at Glacier National Park is part of a global pattern. Glaciers are retreating worldwide. Thirty years from now, I want my grandchildren to live in a world that is safer from disease, freer from droughts and floods, able to grow the food they need for their children and families. But just as importantly, I want them to understand that God created only one earth and that its parks and forests and wilderness preserves can never be replicated. Our responsibility to this land is one of the most profound and sacred responsibilities we have. It is really a responsibility to each other—and to future generations."

—speech at Glacier National Park, Montana,
September 2, 1997

"The environment faces dire threats from the kind of legislation that Senator [Robert] Dole and Speaker Newt Gingrich tried to pass by shutting down the government and attempting to force President Clinton to accept it. They invited the lobbyists for the biggest polluters in America to come into the Congress and literally rewrite the Clean Water Act and the Clean Air Act. President Clinton stopped them dead in their tracks."

—vice-presidential debate, St. Petersburg, Florida,
October 9, 1996

"The [Clinton] administration, in part because of my urging and advocacy, has been the most active in protecting the environment of any administration in history, with the possible exception of Teddy Roosevelt. We have protected the Everglades and Yellowstone and the California desert. We have toughened the standards for clean air and for clean water."

—*Outside*, August 2000

"I will not go along with an agenda that is of Big Oil, by Big Oil, and for Big Oil."

—presidential campaign speech in Hollywood, Maryland,
September 21, 2000

"I was in the White House for eight years and I saw the limitations of even the power of the executive branch when the people and their elected representatives in the Congress were not ready to contemplate the big changes that are necessary. [Global warming] is the rare challenge that really has to come from the grass roots up."

—Associated Press, July 7, 2007

"[My] book, *The Assault on Reason*, really came out of my indepth exploration of why it is that this abundant evidence has been so blithely ignored by the political system. Any reasonable person who takes a look at the scientific evidence would have to conclude we face a planetary emergency, and the United States of America has to act quickly and provide moral leadership and political leadership in the world. The fact that it's not happening—yet—says something about the nature of our current decision-making process."

—*The New Republic* online, June 13, 2007

"Scientific warnings about the catastrophic consequences of unchecked global warming were censored by a political appointee in the White House who had no scientific training whatsoever. Today, one of the leading scientific experts in the world on global warming in NASA has been ordered not to talk to members of the press, ordered to keep a careful log of everyone he meets with so that the Executive branch can monitor and control what he shares of his knowledge of global warming. This is a planetary crisis—we owe ourselves a truthful and reasoned discussion."

—speech to the American Constitutional Society,
Washington, D.C., January 16, 2006 (MLK Day)

"It is our time to rise again, to secure our future."

—from *An Inconvenient Truth*

"In the case of the global climate crisis, Bush has publicly demeaned the authors of official scientific reports, by scientists in his administration, that underscore the extreme danger facing the U.S. and the world. And instead, has preferred a crackpot analysis financed by the largest oil company on the planet, ExxonMobil. He even went so far as to censor elements of an EPA report dealing with global warming, and substitute in the official government report language from the crackpot

ExxonMobil report. The consequences of accepting Exxon-
Mobil's advice, that is to do nothing to counter global warming,
are almost literally unthinkable."
—speech at Georgetown University, Washington, D.C.,
October 18, 2004

"*Mother Jones* magazine showed how ExxonMobil, just one
company, has financed in whole or in part 40 different organizations and front groups that exist for the purpose of putting
out disinformation on global warming. I think it's horribly
unethical and immoral. And just as some of the tobacco executives now look back on their efforts in the '70s and '80s and
feel ashamed, I'm certain the day will come when some of
these executives will feel shame about what they're doing
because they have slowed down the ability of our democracy
to absorb the truth of our circumstances."
—*Fresh Air with Terry Gross*, NPR, May 30, 2006

"[The White House] said 'Well, the jury is still out because this
is the first of 21 reports [on climate change] that we have to do.
We really have to wait and do more investigation.' Yes, yes. I
hope he finds the real killer."
—in response to the Commerce Department's report
acknowledging mankind's impact on global warming,
The Stranger (Seattle), June 1, 2006

"All of the important EPA positions have been carefully filled with lawyers and lobbyists representing the worst polluters in their respective industries in order to make sure that those polluters are not inconvenienced by the actual enforcement of the law against excessive pollution."

—speech at Georgetown University, Washington, D.C, October 18, 2004

"Ford and General Motors are now in a state of crisis in the United States because they have missed the long-term shift in consumer preferences and societal preferences toward more efficient automobiles with much less pollution. And the quarterly reports might look good for a little while and then they fall off a cliff."

—BBC Radio 4, February 2, 2006

"Our public discourse is so vulnerable to the kind of rope-a-dope strategies that ExxonMobil and their brethren have been employing for decades now."

—*New York Times,* May 20, 2007

"ExxonMobil is not the correct source of the best scientific information on the climate crisis, even though their views are now dominant in shaping U.S. policy. Our country [blocked] consensus in the G8 meeting on moving aggressively to solve this crisis, the most important challenge we've ever faced."

—*The Tennessean,* June 2, 2007

"ExxonMobil is pretending to say something positive about the environment. They call it 'green-washing.' They are the worst of the opponents when it comes to trying to solve this crisis. They spend millions of dollars a year to spread false information about global warming. It's shocking, really. It's what the tobacco companies did to deceive people about the science connecting smoking with lung disease. It's the same thing."

—*Der Spiegel* (Germany), July 21, 2006

"The United States borrows money from China to buy oil from the Persian Gulf and burn it at home—in ways that destroy the planet."

—*Der Spiegel* (Germany), July 21, 2006

"Just as Enron needed auditors that wouldn't blow the whistle when they lied about future liabilities, Exxon needs a scientific panel that won't blow the whistle on the future damage that will be caused by global warming."

—speech criticizing President Bush for not supporting the re-election of American climate scientist Dr. Robert Watson as head of the Intergovernmental Panel on Climate Change, at Vanderbilt University, Nashville, Tennessee, April 22, 2002 (Earth Day)

"[Global warming] was seen as an arcane, hobby horse issue [in the '90s]. We'll indulge Vice President Gore, and let him do his thing yet again, and then we'll get back to what we know is the serious stuff."

—*New York Times,* May 20, 2007

"It ought to be possible to establish a coordinated global program to accomplish the strategic goal of completely eliminating the internal combustion engine over, say, a 25-year period. It will create more jobs, not destroy jobs."

—from Al Gore's *Earth in the Balance*

Q: Oil and gas are becoming poker chips in a global power game. Dick Cheney just accused Russia of blackmailing Ukraine with its state-owned natural gas monopoly, Gazprom. **A:** He's right about that, but I don't think he really got concerned until some of the oil companies started losing contracts in Russia.

—*Der Spiegel* (Germany), July 21, 2006

"There are many who still do not believe that global warming is a problem at all. And it's no wonder: because they are the targets of a massive and well-organized campaign of disinformation lavishly funded by polluters who are determined to prevent any action to reduce the greenhouse gas emissions that cause global warming out of a fear that their profits might be affected if they had to stop dumping so much pollution into the atmosphere."

—speech to MoveOn.org, New York City, January 14, 2004

"We need a 'carbon freeze'. I intend to launch an ongoing campaign of mass persuasion at the beginning of 2007. We need a mass movement in the United States. It ought to start at the grass roots."

—remarks at the Greentech Innovation Network, San Francisco, November 12, 2006

"Once upon a time, your refrigerator could kill you. Early models used toxic and explosive gases to keep food cold. In 1927, chlorofluorocarbons (CFCs) replaced those gases. But in 1974, scientists theorized that as CFCs rose into the upper atmosphere, their molecules would be broken down by the sun, releasing chlorine into the ozone layer and setting in motion a dangerous chain reaction. Ozone protects us from the sun's damaging rays. In 1987, 27 nations signed the Montreal Protocol, the first global environmental agreement to regulate CFCs. At last count there were 183 signatories, and the levels of CFCs have stabilized or declined. Today, as the CO_2 crisis unites us, we must remember the lesson of the CFC battle: that cool heads can prevail and alter the course of environmental change for the better."

—from *An Inconvenient Truth* (book)

"It is time for a national oil change. That is apparent to anyone who has looked at our national dipstick."

—speech at NYU School of Law, New York City,
September 18, 2006

"Our continued dependence of imported oil is connected to the same pattern that leads us to put 70 million tons of global warming pollution into the earth's atmosphere every 24 hours around the world, as if it was an open sewer. And pretending that that doesn't have consequence, when there's signs to tell us it definitely does and we've got stop doing, that's really the essence of this problem. But because it's so pervasive, in order to change it, we really have to have a sea change in public opinion in this country and around the world before the politicians and the government leaders in every nation will have the courage to do what really is necessary."

—*CNN Larry King Live,* July 5, 2007

Q: Regarding gas prices—Do you think that this is purely a supply-and-demand question or do you suspect price gouging? **A:** One of the most insidious parts of it is not only that the prices go up for people who are really hit hard by it, but just when the country gets to the point where we're willing to go whole hog on alternative energy, they manage to bring the price back down again, just below the level where people are outraged enough to go full blast on cellulosic ethanol [an alternative fuel manufactured from biomass] and the other substitutes.

—*The Stranger* (Seattle), June 1, 2006

"We may have no more than 10 years before we cross a point of no return. The world wouldn't end the next day, but if [the scientists] are right, and I believe they are, that would mean that the process of destruction and disintegration of the integrity of the earth's ecological system that supports human civilization would deteriorate and would be irretrievable."

—*CNN Larry King Live*, June 13, 2006

Q: Some Republicans would call you a tree-hugger who's out of touch with the problems of middle-class Americans.

A: First of all, it's a myth to say that you have to choose between the environment and the economy. There are billions of dollars being made by companies introducing solutions to this crisis. The old patterns aren't that enjoyable anyway: sitting in traffic jams, breathing smog. I would like to have light rail systems and comfortable mass transit. We can improve the quality of life, create more jobs and raise incomes as we clean up the environment. Look at the automobile industry: The Republicans and others have argued that we in the U.S. should have the worst standards for fuel efficiency in the world in order to help General Motors and Ford. What's happening to GM and Ford? And companies that are doing well are companies like Toyota. Every Prius (hybrid car) they're doing has a long waiting list.

—*Der Spiegel* (Germany), July 21, 2006

"We're not going to solve this problem by buying Priuses and changing our light bulbs. But driving hybrids and choosing better technology is still important in two respects. First, it makes a small contribution to reducing CO_2. And second, when people make changes in their own lives, they are much more likely to become part of a critical mass of public opinion and to support the bigger policy changes that are going to be needed to really solve the problem."

—*Rolling Stone*, June 12–28, 2007

"This is a moral moment. This is not ultimately about any scientific debate or political dialogue. Ultimately it is about who we are as human beings."

—speech to the Sierra Summit, San Francisco, September 9, 2005

"A huge area of snow near the South Pole, an area the size of California, has been melting. The scientists are practically screaming from the rooftops on this."

—*The Early Show*, July 6, 2007

"If we did not take action to solve this crisis, it could indeed threaten the future of human civilization. That sounds shrill. It sounds hard to accept. I believe it's deadly accurate. But again, we can solve it."

—*CNN Larry King Live*, June 13, 2006

"Sixty years ago, Winston Churchill wrote about another kind of gathering storm. When Neville Chamberlain tried to wish [the Nazi] threat away with appeasement, Churchill said, 'This is only the beginning of the reckoning. This is only the first sip, the first foretaste, of a bitter cup which will be proffered to us year by year—unless by a supreme recovery of moral health and martial vigor, we rise again and take our stand for freedom.'"

—Al Gore, "The Time to Act is Now," *Rolling Stone*, November 3, 2005

"Global warming pollution, indeed all pollution, is now described by economists as an 'externality.' This absurd label means, in essence: we don't keep track of this stuff so let's pretend it doesn't exist."

—speech at NYU School of Law, New York City, September 19, 2006

"Hydrogen may be the ultimate clean fuel of the future. But most experts agree that a hydrogen economy is at least a few decades away. But cracking the hydrogen out of coal or natural gas produces a stream of almost pure carbon dioxide, which—unless locked away—could make the greenhouse effect worse."

—from *An Inconvenient Truth* (book)

"There is no longer any serious debate over the basic points that make up the consensus on global warming. The ten warmest years on record have all been since 1990. Globally, 2005 was the hottest of all. In the United States; 2006 was the warmest year ever. The winter months of December 2006 through February 2007 make up the warmest winter on record."

—testimony before the U.S. House of Representatives Subcommittee on Energy & Environment, March 21, 2007

"In the last six years, we have been able to stop global warming. No one could have predicted the negative results of this. Glaciers that once were melting are now on the attack. As you know, these renegade glaciers have already captured parts of upper Michigan and northern Maine. But I assure you, we will not let the glaciers win."

—mock-addressing the nation as if he were president on *Saturday Night Live*, May 13, 2006

"Farmers are the first environmentalists. And when they decide not to plow a field that is vulnerable to soil erosion, that may cost them a little money, but it helps the environment. We ought to have an expanded conservation reserve program. The environmental benefits that come from sound management of the land ought to represent a new way for farmers to get some income that will enable them to make sensible choices in crop rotation and when you leave the land fallow and the rest."

—presidential debate, St. Louis, October 17, 2000

"Our [Clinton-Gore] administration's goal is to triple the use of biomass technologies, ethanol, gasoline additives, plant-based textiles and other environmentally friendly products by 2010. This is just one of the exciting ways our efforts to protect the environment will begin to help America's ailing farming economy."

—reported by the Sustainable Energy Coalition, November 18, 1999

"When acid rain was falling on parts of the U.S. back in the 1980s, an innovative program helped to clean up the polluted precipitation. With bipartisan support, Congress put in place a system for buying and selling emissions of sulfur dioxide (SO_2), the main culprit behind acid rain. Called a cap-and-trade system, it used the power of market forces to help drastically reduce SO_2 emissions, while allowing pioneering companies to profit from environmental stewardship."

—from *An Inconvenient Truth* (book)

"There will be no shortage of statements from Mother Nature."
—*Rolling Stone*, June 12–28, 2007

"Abraham Maslow, best known for his hierarchy of needs, had a dictum that if the only tool you use is a hammer, then every problem begins to look like a nail. Translating that into this discussion: If the only tool you use for measuring value is a price tag or monetization, then those values that are not easily monetized begin to look like they have no value. And so there's an easy contempt, which they summon on a moment's notice for tree-huggers or people concerned about global warming."
—*New Yorker*, September 13, 2004

"Our environment is under siege. There is a movement afoot by polluters to dismantle Americans' capacity to limit their releases of dangerous waste products. When it comes to energy and environmental policy, the Bush administration has brought the oil company representatives out of the lobby and into the Oval Office and let them rewrite America's environmental laws during secret meetings. Their first order of business was to withdraw from the global agreement reached in Kyoto [Japan], to begin limiting worldwide emissions of greenhouse gases."
—speech at Vanderbilt University, Nashville,
April 22, 2002 (Earth Day)

"Our natural role is to be the pace car in the race to stop global warming."
—quoted from speech at New York School of Law,
New York City, September 18, 2006

"Unbelievable tragedies have been unfolding in the part of Africa near Lake Chad. The region-wide drought has contributed to the famine conditions that put millions at risk. A little discussed contributing factor to the famine and genocide is the disappearance of Lake Chad. Just 40 years ago Lake Chad was as large as Lake Erie—formerly the 6th largest lake in the world. But now due to declining rainfall and ever-intensifying human use, it has shrunk to 1/20th of its original size. The lake's dissipation has led to collapsing fisheries and crops. While Lake Chad withered, intense drought set the stage for the violence that erupted in neighboring Darfur. The more we understand about climate change, the more it looks as if we may be the real culprit— the U.S. emits one-quarter of the world's greenhouse gases. We helped manufacture the suffering in Africa, and we have a moral obligation to try to fix it."
—from *An Inconvenient Truth* (book)

"It's crucial that we not fool ourselves into thinking that we can adapt to this climate crisis. If we don't begin to sharply reduce CO_2 emissions, then there would be no adaptation to the constant reshuffling of the climate deck—rainfall and storms and sea level and soil moisture and diseases and ice melting and all the rest. It would be a different planet from the one on which human beings evolved."

—*Rolling Stone,* June 12–28, 2007

"In the months following the release of *An Inconvenient Truth,* I began to focus on why our democracy has been so slow to deal with the climate crisis. The unwillingness to solve this problem is not only the result of a lack of political will, but it has also been caused by the emergence of a new political environment dangerously hostile to reason, knowledge, and facts. In the long-term, this poses a threat to the very basis of American democracy: the ability of a well-informed citizenry to use the rule of reason to hold government accountable."

—from AlGore.com blog entry, May 22, 2007

"A recent study published by the University of Alaska-Fairbanks indicate that methane is leaking from the Siberian permafrost at five times the predicted levels. Methane is 23 times as potent as greenhouse gas as carbon dioxide and there are billions of tons underneath the permafrost."
—testimony before the U.S. House of Representatives Subcommittee on Energy & Environment, March 21, 2007

"I do not believe that the climate crisis should be a partisan political issue. The Tory and Labour parties [in the United Kingdom] are in vigorous competition with one another—competing to put forward the best solution to the climate crisis. I look forward to the day when we return to this way of thinking here in the U.S."
—testimony before the U.S. House of Representatives Subcommittee on Energy & Environment, March 21, 2007

"The evangelical and faith communities have begun to take the lead, calling for measures to protect God's creation."

"Our brains are much better at perceiving danger in fangs and claws and spiders and fire. It's more difficult to trigger the alarm parts of the brain—those connected to survival—with grave dangers that can only be perceived through abstract models and complex data."

—*Rolling Stone*, July 13–27, 2006

"As to why there are still skeptics [about global warming]—there are people who believe that the moon landing was staged in a movie lot in Arizona. Another reason is that some of the largest polluters are still putting millions of dollars a year to hire pseudo scientists to confuse people into thinking that this crisis isn't real."

—*Time*, November 27, 2006

"What the scientists are saying when they give this dark warning is that we may have as little as ten years before we cross a tipping point, beyond which there's an irretrievable process of degradation. They are saying that we have to make a large, good-faith start—to first reduce the amount of global-warming pollution, and then eventually to flatten it and turn it down. It is very possible to start leveling it out within the next five years."

—*Rolling Stone*, July 13–27, 2006

"The rapid urbanization of the world's population is leading to the prospective development of more new urban buildings in the next 35 years than have been constructed in all previous human history. This startling trend represents a tremendous opportunity for sharp reductions in global warming pollution through the use of intelligent architecture and design and stringent standards. We should create a Carbon Neutral Mortgage Association to market these new financial instruments and stimulate their use in the private sector by utilities, banks and homebuilders. This new 'Connie Mae' (CNMA) could be a valuable instrument for reducing the pollution from new buildings."

—speech at New York University School of Law, New York City, September 18, 2006

"For the last fourteen years, I have advocated the elimination of all payroll taxes—including those for Social Security and unemployment compensation—and the replacement of that revenue in the form of pollution taxes—principally on CO_2. The overall level of taxation would remain exactly the same. It would be, in other words, a revenue-neutral tax swap. But, instead of discouraging businesses from hiring more employees, it would discourage business from producing more pollution. Penalizing pollution instead of penalizing employment will work to reduce that pollution."

—speech at New York University School of Law, New York City, September 18, 2006

"In developing countries, with growing populations and crowded cities, the air pollution and water pollution burdens are far worse than what we experience. Their governments are eager to gain access to a new generation of technologies that will allow improvements in the standard of living for their people, while actually reducing the burden of pollution."

—*Outside*, August 2000

"The environment used to be a bipartisan issue. It's relatively new to have almost the entire Republican Party adopt an aggressive anti-environmentalist stance, even though the rank-and-file Republican voters don't feel that way."

—*Outside*, August 2000

"We were warned of an imminent attack by Al Qaeda; we didn't respond. We were warned the levees would break in New Orleans; we didn't respond. Now, the scientific community is warning us that the average hurricane will continue to get stronger because of global warming."

—speech to the Sierra Summit, San Francisco, September 9, 2005

"I talked to a CEO of one of the ten largest companies in the United States, who supported Bush and Cheney. He told me, 'Al, let's be honest. Fifteen minutes after George Bush leaves the presidency, America is going to have a new global-warming policy, and it doesn't matter who's elected.'"

—*Rolling Stone*, July 13–27, 2006

"Well, the title *An Inconvenient Truth* is a way of highlighting the reasons why some people, including the president, don't seem to accept the truth. It's inconvenient. This administration, as has been abundantly documented, is quite responsive to the oil and coal industry and, by the way, to the least responsible companies within those industries. And they do not want anything done on global warming."

—*Newsweek*, April 28, 2006

"Two years ago we became a carbon-neutral family. I purchase Green Power [electricity from renewable sources], have installed new light bulbs and clock thermostats, and I'm installing solar panels. We switched to a hybrid car. I am not recommending actions that I haven't already taken myself."

—*Time*, November 27, 2006

"Paper, glass, cans. And we recycle in my home. I can't take credit for my family getting into that because my children led the way on that. But one of the reasons I wrote *Earth in the Balance* is to put in one place all the facts for anybody who is curious about why their kids are so involved in this issue and what families can do to address the issue."

—*Booknotes,* February 16, 1992

Q: All right. We have an e-mail from Jerry in Houston, Texas. "Mr. Gore, how can you fly in your private jet, live in a massive mansion and set an example for others?"

A: Well, first of all, I fly commercial most of the time. There are a few occasions when that's not possible. I came here on a commercial airliner and we just finished putting 33 solar photovoltaic cells on the roof of our house. We're right now in the midst of installing a geothermal system for the heating and cooling and changing the remaining lights and windows and insulation that haven't already been done and we are walking the walk and we're going to have a green standard, the lead certification, for our house. I drive a hybrid and all the rest and look, I've never claimed to be perfect but I'm doing the best I can and one of the pledges at the Live Earth concerts—the second pledge—is to reduce my own global warming pollution as much as I can and offset the rest in order to become carbon neutral.

—*CNN Larry King Live,* July 5, 2007

"Many people seem to be largely oblivious of this collision [between human civilization and the natural world] and the addictive nature of our unhealthy relationship to the earth. But education is a cure for those who lack knowledge; much more worrisome are those who will not acknowledge these destructive patterns. Indeed, many political, business, and intellectual leaders deny the existence of any such patterns in aggressive and dismissive tone. They serve as 'enablers' removing inconvenient obstacles and helping to ensure that the addictive behavior continues."

—from Al Gore's *Earth in the Balance*

"*An Inconvenient Truth* isn't a political film. Global warming isn't a political issue. It's about the survival of the planet. Nobody is going to care who won or lost any election when the earth is uninhabitable."

—*Entertainment Weekly,* July 13, 2006

"1. To demand that my country join an international treaty within the next two years that cuts global warming pollution by 90 percent in developed countries and by more than half worldwide in time for the next generation to inherit a healthy earth; 2. To take personal action to help solve the climate crises by reducing my own CO_2 pollution as much as I can and offsetting the rest to become 'carbon neutral'; 3. To fight for a moratorium on the construction of any new generating facility that burns coal without the capacity to safely trap and store the CO_2; 4. To work for a dramatic increase in the energy efficiency of my home, workplace, school, place of worship, and means of transportation; 5. To fight for laws and policies that expand the use of renewable energy sources and reduce dependence on oil and coal; 6. To plant new trees and to join with others in preserving and protecting forests; and, 7. To buy from businesses and support leaders who share my commitment to solving the climate crises and building a sustainable, just and prosperous world for the 21st century."

—Al Gore's "Seven Point Pledge," Associated Press,
June 28, 2007

"Americans must come together and direct our government to take on a global challenge. To this end, we should demand that the United States join an international treaty within the next two years that cuts global warming pollution by 90 percent in developed countries and by more than half worldwide in time for the next generation to inherit a healthy Earth."

—Al Gore's op-ed "Moving Beyond Kyoto,"
New York Times, July 1, 2007

"The planet doesn't have a PR agent. But now it will, because the Alliance for Climate Protection is going to use the modern techniques of messaging to get the scientific evidence in front of people all over the world."

—Associated Press, July 7, 2007

"I promise you a day will come when our children and our grandchildren will look back, and they'll ask one of two questions. Either they will ask, 'What in God's name were they doing? Didn't they see the evidence? Didn't they realize that four times in 15 years the entire scientific community of this world issued unanimous reports calling on them to act? What was wrong with them?' Or they'll ask another question. They may look back and they may say, 'How did they find the uncommon moral courage to rise above politics and redeem the promise of American democracy, and do what some said was impossible?'"

—testimony before the U.S. House of Representatives
Subcommittee on Energy & Environment,
March 21, 2007

"There's an old cliché about the way the Chinese write the word 'crisis.' They have two symbols back to back. The first means danger, and the second means opportunity. We should feel a great sense of urgency because [global warming] is the most dangerous crisis we have ever faced. But it also provides us with opportunities to do a lot of things we ought to be doing for other reasons anyway."

—CNN *Larry King Live,* June 13, 2006

THE 2000 PRESIDENTIAL RACE

"I think all elections for president in this country are about our nation's soul."

—Town Hall Meeting, Nashua, New Hampshire, December 18, 1999

"Polls don't win elections. Ideas do."

—March, 2000

"I helped to pass the toughest new gun control measures in a generation. I believe that we ought to have total license IDs for the purchase of new handguns. I think we ought to ban assault weapons and Saturday night specials and junk guns. I also am committed to the principle of high quality affordable health care for all. And I don't really care what kind of label people apply to those positions and views."

—Democratic primary debate in
Durham, New Hampshire, January 5, 2000

"I cast the tie-breaking vote to close the so-called gun show loophole. The NRA has targeted me as a result. We have got to take them on strongly and pass new gun control legislation— not aimed at hunters and sportsmen, but at these handguns that are causing so much distress in our country."

—Democratic primary debate in Los Angeles, March 1, 2000

"The government's role should not be to regulate content, obviously. The government should give parents more tools to protect their young children, give citizens more protections against violations of privacy. We should keep the moratorium on taxing transactions on the Internet while the questions are dealt with. And we've got to close the digital divide so that everybody, regardless of income or social circumstances has access to the Internet."

—Democratic primary debate in Los Angeles, March 1, 2000

Q: What would you do to bring down gas prices?

A: To put in place a program called the Partnership for a New Generation of Vehicles, which commits the big three auto makers in our country to getting new vehicles into the marketplace that have three times the efficiency of today's vehicles. That's part of the answer.

—Democratic primary debate in Los Angeles, March 1, 2000

"We should allow more immigrants to come [into our country]. We are a nation of immigrants and with pride. It is what has made us a great nation. All of us, save the Native Americans, need only count back the generations to find when our families immigrated here or when they were brought here in chains."

—Democratic primary debate in Los Angeles, March 1, 2000

"Social Security is a solemn compact. Its basic guarantee of retirement security is based on its guaranteed minimum benefit. To turn Social Security into a system of winners and losers would jeopardize Social Security for all Americans. Governor Bush's plan takes the 'security' out of Social Security."

—CNN.com, May 15, 2000

"I will preserve these roadless areas [in the Tongass National Forest in Alaska, the nation's largest] as they are, no ifs, ands or buts about it. No more destructive development. No new road-building and no timber sales in the roadless areas. Period."

—*New York Times*, May 31, 2000

"The fundamental choice has to do with whose side are you on. I want to fight for the people; the other side fights for the powerful. That's why the big pharmaceutical companies are supporting Governor Bush. That's why the big oil companies are supporting Governor Bush. That's why the big polluters are supporting Governor Bush. That's why the HMOs and insurance companies are supporting Governor Bush."

—*New York Times*, July 7, 2000

"I am going to be running with the teachers and the farmers and the bus drivers and the hard working men and women of this country. I'm going to be running with the people, not the privileged."

—CNN.com, July 26, 2000

"I'm running on my own agenda, on my own voice and through my own experiences. President Clinton gave us a foundation upon which I will build. The proposals I'm making for the future are rooted in my 24-year fight for working families. My passion for protecting the environment is rooted in the battle that I've waged for almost a quarter century."

—*New York Times,* August 13, 2000

"I'm not a natural backslapping politician. I need a longer runway to become airborne. In the final three months of this campaign, you won't see many off days."

—*USA Today,* August 16, 2000

"I've cut down on the size of my motorcades quite a bit. But so long as we face the terrorist threat that we do, they insist upon the heavy armored vehicles. They don't come in solar form."

—at a presidential campaign stop in Detroit,
Outside, August 2000

"I will keep America's defenses strong. I will make sure our armed forces continue to be the best-equipped, best-trained, and best-led in the entire world. In the last century, this nation more than any other freed the world from fascism and communism. But a newly free world still has dangers and challenges, both old and new. We must always have the will to defend our enduring interests, and we must strengthen our partnerships with Africa, Latin America, and the rest of the developing world."
—acceptance speech at the Democratic National Convention,
August 16, 2000

"Let me tell you, under the tax plan the other side has proposed, for every $10 that goes to the wealthiest one percent, middle-class families would get one dime, and lower-income families would get one penny. In fact, if you add it up, the average family would get about enough money to buy one extra Diet Coke a week, about—it's not nothing. About 62 cents in change. But let me tell you, that's not the kind of change I'm working for."
—acceptance speech at the Democratic National Convention,
August 16, 2000

"I know my own imperfections. For example, I know that sometimes people say I'm too serious, that I talk too much substance and policy. Maybe I've done that tonight. But the presidency is more than a popularity contest, it's a day-by-day fight for people."
—acceptance speech at the Democratic National Convention,
August 16, 2000

Q: Do you support the "don't ask, don't tell" policy on gays in the military?
A: The "don't ask, don't tell" policy has not worked. Furthermore, I believe that, as a matter of basic fairness, the policy should be changed. It is unacceptable that patriotic men and women who serve their nation with distinction are not only discharged, but suffer persecution and even violence. They should be allowed to serve their country without discrimination.
—*New York Times*, August 23, 2000

"Now, one of the central choices that we face in this election, just 47 days from now, is whether we will have a president who is willing to stand up to the big oil interests and fight for our families; that's the kind of president that I intend to be. I'm running for president to fight for you and to stand up for your interests. You know, we've come a long way in the last eight years, but this election is not an award for past performance. I'm not asking any of you to vote for me on the basis of the economy we have. I ask for your support on the basis of the better, fairer economy and more prosperous America that we can build together. Together, let's make sure that our prosperity enriches not just the few, but all of our families. Let's put more of the power and more of the choices back in your hands. I promise you this: If I am president, I'm going to stand up to Big Oil and demand fair gasoline prices for our families and an end to unfair profiteering. We have to also press OPEC and Big Oil to act responsibly. And we also need aggressive national action right now. So I'm proposing an energy security and environment trust, a commitment to a more prosperous economy powered by cleaner, cheaper, and more reliable energy for families."
  —presidential campaign speech in Hollywood, Maryland,
September 21, 2000

"Governor Bush is proposing to open up some of our most precious environmental treasures, like the Arctic National Wildlife Refuge, to the big oil companies to go in and start producing oil there. I think that is the wrong choice. It would only

give us a few months worth of oil, and the oil wouldn't start flowing for many years into the future. And I don't think it's a fair price to pay, to destroy precious parts of America's environment."
—presidential debate in Boston, October 3, 2000

"Governor [Bush] may want to focus on scandals; I want to focus on results. I stand here as my own man, and I want you to see me for who I really am. I may not be the most exciting politician, but I will work hard for you every day, I will fight for middle class families and working men and women, and I will never let you down. I think the American people should take into account who we are as individuals, what our experience is, and what our proposals are."
—presidential debate in Boston, October 3, 2000

Q: What is your Social Security plan?
A: I will keep it in a lockbox. The interest savings I would put right back into it. That extends the life for 55 years. I am opposed to a plan that diverts one out of every six dollars away from the Trust Fund. It would go bankrupt within this generation. The governor's plan is "Social Security Minus." Your future benefits would be cut by the amount that's diverted into the stock market. And if you make bad investments, that's too bad.
—presidential debate in Boston, October 3, 2000

"I put all my sighs in a lockbox."
—appearing on NBC after the second presidential debate in
Boston, October 3, 2000

"Look, the world's temperature is going up, weather patterns are changing, storms are getting more violent and unpredictable. And what are we going to tell our children?"
—presidential debate in Winston-Salem, North Carolina,
October 11, 2000

"We've made some progress during the last eight years. We have seen the strongest economy in the history of the United States, lower crime rates for eight years in a row, highest private home ownership ever. But I'll make you one promise here: You ain't seen nothing yet. And I will keep that promise."
—presidential debate in St Louis, October 17, 2000

"My plan to put Social Security in an ironclad lockbox has gotten a lot of attention recently, and I'm glad about that. But I'm afraid that it's overshadowing some vitally important proposals. For instance, I'll put Medicaid in a walk-in closet. I'll put the Community Reinvestment Act in a secured gym locker. I'll put NASA funding in a hermetically sealed Ziploc bag."

—speech at the Al Smith Dinner in New York City,
October 19, 2000

"I learned some important lessons in the debates, for example, wearing Estée Lauder makeup is good. Having Ron Lauder actually apply the makeup is bad."

—speech at the Al Smith Dinner in New York City,
October 19, 2000

"Incidentally, it's not true that I've agreed to sell ad space during my speeches. By the way, have I mentioned that the 2000 Buick LeSabre is the smoothest ride this side of heaven? This is a fundraiser isn't it? Whenever I see everybody dressed the same way, my antenna goes straight up."

—speech at the Al Smith Dinner in New York City,
October 19, 2000

"When it comes to the environment, I've never given up, I've never turned back, and I never will."

—campaign speech in Portland, Oregon, October 23, 2000

"Governor Bush often says you should support him because he'd get along with people in Washington, and that's all well and good and we certainly need less partisanship. But the real question is, who does he want to get along with? The special interests who want to see more massive tax giveaways to the wealthiest? The powerful interests who always come out ahead and block our greatest chance to make this prosperity work for you?"

—from Gore campaign, November 2, 2000

"As governor, George W. Bush gave Big Oil a tax break while opposing health care for 220,000 kids. Texas now ranks 50th in family health care. He's left the minimum wage at $3.35 an hour, let polluters police themselves. Today, Texas ranks last in air quality. Now Bush promises the same $1 trillion from Social Security to two different groups. He squanders the surplus on a tax cut for those making over $300,000. Is he ready to lead America?"

—Gore campaign television commercial, November 2, 2000

"Do you want to entrust the Oval Office to somebody who doesn't even know Social Security is a federal program?"

—CNN.com, November 3, 2000

"Wake up, it's time to take your souls to the polls!"

—speech in Nashville, Tennessee, November 4, 2000

"I don't like the argument that a vote for Nader is a vote for Bush, [but] I think it's true. That's why the Republicans are running TV ads for Nader."

—November 7, 2000

"Running for president is a hell of lot different than speaking as a vice president, where you are constantly mindful of how to push the administration's agenda forward."

—*Rolling Stone,* November 9, 2000

"I'm certain there were times when some people in the [2000 presidential] campaign said, 'Oh no, he wants to talk about the global environment again, and that's not going to get us anywhere.' But that is just a grain of truth—it's not the truth. My perception is that I talked about it frequently, at length. But the media was less than convinced that global warming was a legitimate issue. They said, 'It's odd that he's talking about this.' And now, after the fact, they say, 'I don't remember him talking about it.' Well, hello?"

—*New York,* May 22, 2006

Q: What did you think during the 2000 campaign on the day that Bush announced he would limit CO_2 emissions if he were elected?

A: I thought it was fraudulent. I actually did not anticipate that he would directly and brazenly break that pledge, and go 180 degrees in the opposite direction at full speed, but I thought that he would slow-walk it and make it meaningless. They were trying to drain the moral energy out of an issue that they felt could hurt them if the public perceived a clear contrast on the issue.

—*Rolling Stone*, July 13–27, 2006

ELECTION DAY 2000—THE AFTERMATH

"That is all we have asked since Election Day: a complete count of all the votes cast in Florida. Not recount after recount as some have charged, but a single, full, and accurate count. We haven't had that yet. Great efforts have been made to prevent the counting of these votes. Lawsuit after lawsuit has been filed to delay the count and to stop the counting for many precious days between Election Day and the deadline for having the count finished. And this would be over long since, except for those efforts to block the process at every turn. Many thousands of votes that were cast on Election Day have not yet been counted at all, not once. There are some who would have us bring this election to the fastest conclusion possible. I have a different view. I believe our Constitution matters more than convenience."

—speech on prime-time national television,
November 27, 2000

Q: Why not just come out and turn the tables on them and say, "I believe I won the election. And I believe they are trying to steal the election"?

A: Well, I've never used the phrase "steal the election." I think that's an intemperate phrase. And I think that both Governor Bush and I have an obligation during this period when the votes are yet to be counted to try to pave the way for whichever one of us wins to be able to unify the country. The only way to avoid having a cloud over the next president is to count all the votes. Because our country is based on the consent of the governed.

—CNN interview, November 29, 2000

"Regardless of how [the election] comes out, whoever is sworn in as president on January 20th, should have the support of all the people, and if that's not me, I will not question the fairness or legitimacy of the final outcome."

—*60 Minutes*, December 3, 2000

"And on January 20th, if the person standing up before the Capitol taking the oath of office is George Bush and not me, he will be sworn in as my president, too, and I will spare no efforts in saying to people who supported me, let's not have any talk about stealing the election."

—*60 Minutes*, December 3, 2000

"Over the library of one of our great law schools is inscribed the motto, 'Not under man but under God and law.' That's the ruling principle of American freedom, the source of our democratic liberties. I've tried to make it my guide throughout this contest as it has guided America's deliberations of all the complex issues of the past five weeks. Now the U.S. Supreme Court has spoken. Let there be no doubt, while I strongly disagree with the court's decision, I accept it. I accept the finality of this outcome."

> —televised presidential concession speech,
> December 13, 2000

"I do believe as my father once said, that no matter how hard the loss, defeat might serve as well as victory to shape the soul and let the glory out."

> —televised presidential concession speech,
> December. 13, 2000

"It was a crushing disappointment. I believe that if everyone in Florida who tried to vote had had his or her vote counted properly, that I would have won. I strongly disagreed with the Supreme Court decision, and the way in which they interpreted and applied the law. But I respect the rule of law, so it is what it is. Look, the other guy was sworn in. End of story."

> —*Washington Post,* November 17, 2002

"I'm not sure I'm able to find the words to describe what I was feeling. [It was] like 'hand-to-hand combat.'"

—describing the 36-day post-election period,
Washington Post, November 17, 2002

"I'm a visiting professor now, or VP, for short. It's a way of hanging on."

—*Washington Post,* November 17, 2002

"I was surprised that the [Supreme Court] took the case. I was shocked because the philosophy that had been followed by the conservative majority on the court was completely inconsistent with a decision to take the case away from the state court. After the shock and surprise, I just shifted into trying to respond in the most effective way I could, with the right legal talent, adequate resources. I don't know. I'm kind of task-oriented. I sort of focused on how to overcome. I held out every hope that the court would do what I personally felt was the right thing. I had tried to prepare both myself and my family for the eventuality that it would not come out our way. We had prayed together frequently as a family that we would not be vulnerable to bitterness. We tried to reach out for a higher plane."

—*Washington Post,* November 17, 2002

Q: Had you been elected president, how might U.S. policy vis à vis Israel and Palestine, Iraq, Afghanistan and the Middle East generally be different than it is today? [Audience members: "You were elected!"]

A: So when people say, "You were elected," I say well, you know, there's something missing here. I was in Florida last week. Did y'all notice that there was an election there last week? Jay Leno said he sent an investigative team from *The Tonight Show*, and they discovered that the problem was that all the voting machines were still clogged with Gore-Lieberman ballots. I've tried to avoid this business of saying what I would have done differently from the president in the run-up to September 11. But I will single out one thing that I think should have been done very differently. Once we pushed the Taliban out of power, I believe that we should have had a force of 30,000 to 35,000 international troops to come into Afghanistan and do like we did in Bosnia, and say, "Okay, y'all, there's a new sheriff in town, and just calm down." And after a while their blood pressure goes down and after a while their general expectation of violence and conflict is replaced with a general expectation of cooperation. That was not done in Afghanistan. Many in our military advised that it be done. Many people close to the president, I read, advised that it be done. I don't know why it wasn't done.

—remarks following speech at
the Commonwealth Club,
San Francisco, September 23, 2002

"After twenty-four years and thirty-six days in public service, I wanted to take some time off."

—*NPR Morning Edition*, November 21, 2002

"The country went through quite a traumatic experience in that thirty-six-day recount period and the new president needed the affirmation of legitimacy. I could have run a four-year rear-guard guerrilla campaign to undermine his legitimacy . . . [but] with the United States as the acknowledged leader of the world, I personally came to the conclusion that in accepting the rule of law I also wanted to accept an obligation to withdraw from the public stage for a time."

—*NPR Morning Edition*, November 21, 2002

"We would not have invaded a country that did not attack us. We would not have taken money from the working families and given it to the most wealthy families. We would not be trying to control and intimidate the news media. We would not be routinely torturing people."

—talking to reporters in Sweden on how the U.S. would have been different if he had won the 2000 election, October 24, 2005

"The good news about not being President is that I have my weekends free. The bad news is that my weekdays are also free. But I just want to say at the outset, tonight is not about rehashing things from the past. I mean, we all know there are things I should have done differently in the 2000 campaign. Maybe at times I was too wooden and stiff and I sighed too much and people said I was too patronizing. Patronizing, of course, means talking to people like they're stupid."

—as guest host on *Saturday Night Live*, December 14, 2002

"My friends, fellow Democrats, fellow Americans: I'm going to be candid with you. I had hoped to be back here this week under different circumstances, running for re-election. But you know the old saying—'You win some, you lose some. And then there's that little-known third category.' I didn't come here tonight to talk about the past. After all, I don't want you to think I lie awake at night counting and recounting sheep. I prefer to focus on the future, because I know from my own experience that America is a land of opportunity, where every little boy and girl has a chance to grow up and win the popular vote."

—speech at the 2004 Democratic National Convention, July 26, 2004

"The first lesson is this: Take it from me, every vote counts."
—speech at the 2004 Democratic
National Convention, July 26, 2004

"They look at these speeches pretty closely. They don't want any Bush-bashing in there. No Bush-bashing at the Democratic Convention! It reminds me of the time Steve Martin was giving a speech in honor of Paul Simon at the Kennedy Center a couple of years ago, and he said, 'It would be easy to stand here and talk about Paul Simon's intelligence and skill, but this is neither the time *nor* the place."
—discussing 2004 Democratic National Convention
speech policies, *New Yorker*, September 13, 2004

"I am concerned about the economy. I was the first one laid off. It's true that along with all the jobs lost, there are some new jobs being created, but the new jobs aren't as good as the ones that people have lost and that's true for me, too."
—debate with Senator Robert Dole at Regent University,
Virginia Beach, Virginia, October 25, 2004

"I am supporting the Kerry-Edwards ticket and you also know that I am biased against George W. Bush. I didn't vote for the guy."
—debate with Senator Robert Dole at Regent University, Virginia Beach, Virginia, October 25, 2004

"I think it was a tough [2000 presidential campaign] environment. It's now clear that a fairly significant recession started in the spring of the election year, and the stock market fell dramatically all through the campaign, and it came at the end of an eight-year cycle that triggered the normal pendulum effect of American politics—which cuts in two different ways. The hunger of the party that's been satiated for eight years has a half-life. And the hunger and determination of the party that's been out for eight years is built up to a fevered pitch. And then there's a third factor. In both 1992 and 1996, Bill Clinton and I were very fortunate to have a significant third-party candidate that drew virtually all of his votes from the Republican nominee. By contrast, in 2000, there was a third-party candidate drawing from me. And the task of holding down that number to the noise level, while simultaneously reaching out to the centrist voters who were vulnerable to that pendulum effect, made it a campaign of an impressive degree of difficulty. In spite of that, we won the popular vote and came within one Supreme Court justice's vote of winning the election. So if that final decision had gone the other way, the question might well be, how did you guys pull it off?"
—New York, May 22, 2006

"Not long ago, I was on Interstate 40 going from here [Nashville] to Carthage, Tennessee. [Tipper and I] were driving ourselves. I looked in the rearview mirror. There was no motorcade. You heard of phantom-limb pain?"

—*New Yorker,* September 13, 2004

"Soon after Tipper and I left the White House we were driving from our home in Nashville to a little farm we have fifty miles east of Nashville. It was dinner time and we started looking for a place to eat. We got to exit 238, Lebanon, Tennessee. We got off the exit, starting looking, found a Shoney's restaurant. Low-cost family restaurant chain for those of you who don't know it. We went in and sat down at the booth and the waitress came over and made a big commotion over Tipper. She took our order and then went to the couple in the booth next to us and she lowered her voice so much I had to really strain to hear what she was saying. And she said, 'Yes, that's former Vice President Al Gore and his wife, Tipper,' and the man said, 'He's come down a long way, hasn't he.'"

—speech at TED Talks, Monterey, CA, June 27, 2006

"Four years and four months ago, the Supreme Court of the United States, in a bitterly divided 5 to 4 decision, issued an unsigned opinion that the majority cautioned should never be used as a precedent for any subsequent case anywhere in the federal court system. Even though many of my supporters said they were unwilling to accept a ruling which they suspected was brazenly partisan in its motivation and simply not entitled to their respect, less than 24 hours later, I went before the American people to reaffirm the bedrock principle that we are a nation of laws, not men. The demonstrators and counter-demonstrators left the streets and the nation moved on—as it should have—to accept the inauguration of George W. Bush as our 43rd president."

—speech to MoveOn.org, Washington, D.C., April 27, 2005

"I'm willing to bear my responsibility for not being more effective as a communicator."

—*Charlie Rose*, May 25, 2007

"I think non-candidates are inherently more popular than candidates."

—GQ, December 2006

"I've chosen not to challenge the rule of law because in our system there really is no intermediate step between a final Supreme Court decision and violent revolution."

—*Charlie Rose*, May 25, 2007

"I've fallen out of love with politics. I miss some things, but there is a lot I don't miss at all."

—*The Guardian* (UK), June 2, 2007

Q: Was the [2000] election stolen?

A: There may come a time when I speak on that, but it's not now; I need more time to frame it carefully if I do.

—*New York*, May 22, 2006

TO SERVE ONE'S COUNTRY

"I think that I have learned a few things in the last six years, but there is no question that it is a luxury to be able to focus on one huge issue."
—speaking about global warming in *The Guardian* (UK),
June 2, 2007

"Early to bed, early to rise, work like hell and organize."
—during his first run for U.S. president
at the age of thirty-nine, in 1988

"I've seen America in this campaign and I like what I see. It's worth fighting for and that's a fight I'll never stop."
—televised presidential concession speech, December 13, 2000

"I left Harvard in 1969 disillusioned by what I saw happening in our country and certain of only one thing about my future: I would never, ever go into politics. After returning from Vietnam and after seven years as a journalist, I rekindled my interest in public service."

—Harvard Commencement Day Address, June 9, 1994

"[I went to divinity school] to intensively explore the questions I had which seemed then and seem now to be the most important questions about what's the purpose of life, what's our relationship to the Creator, what's our spiritual obligation to one another. I didn't find all the answers that I thought I might, but I found better questions, and I found a process for living out better answers."

—New York Times, May 29, 1999

"Tipper and I are giving 100 percent of all the profits we get from both the movie and the book to a new bipartisan alliance for climate protection. It will run ads about the nature of the crisis and the way we can solve it."

—Rolling Stone, July 13–27, 2006

"I am a raging moderate."

—first voiced in 1987

"My father told me, 'Son, you have to pick the walls you're going to butt your head against.' So I use the 'strict scrutiny' standard that I learned in law school about how the Supreme Court uses a different standard for very important cases. I try to be ferocious in defending what's most important to me— freedom of speech, religion—and refused to yield an inch on prayer in school even though 90 percent in my district felt the other way."

—*New York Times,* July 11, 2000

"My mother was born into a poor family here in West Tennessee—at a time when poor girls weren't supposed to dream. And in her words, 'it never occurred to me that I couldn't go to college. I just knew it was up to me to find a way.' She got a $100 loan from the Jackson Rotary Club— which she later repaid. She enrolled at Union in the fall of 1931, waiting tables at Miss Snipes' Restaurant in downtown Jackson to help pay her way. But she dreamed of becoming a lawyer. And despite all the obstacles before her, she refused to let go of that dream. So after two years at Union, my mother came to Nashville and enrolled at Vanderbilt Law School. This time, she scraped her way through by waiting tables at the old Andrew Jackson Hotel, working for 25-cent tips.

When my mother graduated from Vanderbilt, it was virtually impossible for a woman to find a legal job in Nashville. So she left for Texarkana, and put up her shingle. The next year, my father persuaded her to come back as his wife. Soon after, he decided to run for Congress in the old Fourth District. Of course, my mother was much more than a campaigner [for him]. She was my father's closest adviser. And when he took tough and controversial positions, such as his strong support for civil rights, and his opposition to the war in Vietnam—positions that caused great tension among their colleagues and friends—she always stood with him. In 1970, after my father lost his Senate seat because he stood up against the Vietnam War, my mother picked up and returned to her legal career—first at a firm she opened with my father, then as the managing partner at a large firm in Washington.

For all my 52 years, my mother has been the greatest teacher I have ever had. She taught me that through quiet dignity and determination, one woman could make all the difference. She taught me that there are no doors that can't be opened—if you work hard enough and knock long enough. She has passed on to me and my children a deep passion for learning—and a deep sense of obligation, to use that knowledge as a force for good in the world. As long as I am privileged to serve this country, I will cherish the lessons she has taught me."

—speech honoring his mother, Pauline LaFon Gore,
Union University, Jackson, Tennessee, April 10, 2000

Q: Comment on your defense of President Clinton during the Monica Lewinsky scandal.

A: I was critical of the President. I also defended the office of the presidency against a thoroughly disproportionate penalty for a serious and reprehensible personal mistake. He should not have been removed from office for that offense. In fighting against [Congressional] efforts to remove him from office and undo the act of the American people in twice electing him, I think I was serving the public interest well.

—Democratic primary debate in Durham, New Hampshire,

January 5, 2000

Q: Did you ever think that there was a point during the Monica Lewinsky scandal and the impeachment process, that you would become president?

A: You mean, that [President Clinton] would have to resign? No, I never thought that. My duty was to the country, and during a time of stress involving the possibility of a change in the presidency, the absolute worst thing that I could have done would have been to pile on, or appear to be trying to aid the forces attempting to push him out of office.

—*Rolling Stone,* November 9, 2000

"Once it is widely accepted, cynicism—the stubborn, unwavering disbelief in the possibility of good—can become a malignant habit in democracy. Cynicism is deadly. It bites everything it can reach—like a dog with a foot caught in a trap. And then it devours itself. It drains us of the will to improve; it diminishes our public spirit; it saps our inventiveness; it withers our souls."

—Harvard Commencement Day Address, June 9, 1994

"I finished college at a time when all that [American values] seemed to be in doubt and our nation's spirit was being depleted. We saw the assassination of our best leaders, appeals to racial backlash, and the first warning signs of Watergate. I remember the conversations I had with Tipper back them, and the doubts we had about the Vietnam War. But I enlisted in the Army, because I knew if I didn't go, someone else in the small town of Carthage, Tennessee, would have to go in my place. I was an Army reporter in Vietnam. When I was there I didn't do the most or run the gravest danger, but I was proud to wear my country's uniform."

—acceptance speech at the Democratic National Convention, August 16, 2000

"I carried a pencil and an M-16 [in Vietnam]. I didn't come face to face with an enemy that had to kill or be killed."

—*USA Today*, August 16, 2000

"I don't pretend that my own military experience [in Vietnam] matches in any way what others here have been through. And my own experiences gave me strong beliefs about America's obligation to keep our national defenses strong. I will make sure that no members of our armed forces ever have to rely on food stamps. Our armed forces should be commemorated on stamps. They shouldn't have to use them to buy groceries."

—*New York Times,* August 23, 2000

"My father, the bravest politician I have ever known, was slandered as unpatriotic because he opposed the Vietnam War and accused of being an atheist because he opposed a Constitutional Amendment to allow government-sponsored prayer in the public schools. I was in the Army at the time—on my way to Vietnam."

—speech at the New School, New York City, February 4, 2004

"I don't want people voting for me because I'm Albert Gore's son."

—spoken to a friend while running for Congress, 1976; from *Inventing Al Gore,* by Bill Turque

"My family and I know the bitterness of defeat. I have a family that teaches you what public service is all about. I consider the office of congressman a sacred trust."
—Primary night victory speech in his first congressional race, 1976; from *Inventing Al Gore,* by Bill Turque

Q: You've got the magical name—Al Gore. Your father was in Congress for thirty-two years. You've got character. You've got no clay feet, no skeletons showing. You're intelligent. You're well-informed. You've got a Vietnam War record. You've been an investigative reporter, and you've got religious coloration. For one year you were a divinity student, and you're a devout Baptist. Are you too good to be true?
A: Well, I don't know . . .
Q: I mean, what's going to happen to you? You say you have no aspirations for a national career.
A: I'm trying to do the best job I can as a senator.
—*One on One with John McLaughlin,* July 18, 1986; from *Inventing Al Gore,* by Bill Turque

"My father was the greatest man I ever knew in my life. Most of you know him for his public service and it could be said of him, in the words of Paul, that this man walked worthy of the vocation wherewith he was called. There were those many,

many who loved him—and there were a few that hated him for the right reasons. It's better to be hated for what you are than to be loved for what you are not. He made decisions in politics that were such that he could come home and explain to his children what he had decided and why. He was of good courage. He strengthened the fainthearted. He supported the weak. He helped the afflicted. He loved and served all people who came his way. None of this was a secret to the world. As most of you know, there was a time where some people thought my father should seek the highest office in the land. Here's what he said about that idea: 'The lure of the presidency never really overwhelmed me, though there were times when the vice president seemed extremely attractive.' The last advice he gave me, two weeks ago, when he was almost too weak to speak, was this: 'Always do right.'"

—eulogy (excerpted) at the funeral of former
Senator Albert Gore, Sr., War Memorial Auditorium,
Nashville, Tennessee, December 8, 1998

"I grew up in a wonderful family. I have a lot to be thankful for. And the greatest gift my parents gave me was love. When I was a child, it never once occurred to me that the foundation upon which my security depended would ever shake. And of all the lessons my parents taught me, the most powerful one was unspoken: The way they loved one another. My father respected my mother as an equal, if not more. She was his best friend, and in many ways, his conscience. And I learned from them the value of a true, loving partnership that lasts for life.

They simply couldn't imagine being without each other, and for 61 years they were by each other's side. My parents taught me that the real values in life aren't material, but spiritual. They include faith and family, duty and honor and trying to make the world a better place."

—acceptance speech at the Democratic National Convention, August 16, 2000

"I believe that a lot of people are skeptical about people in politics today,[but] I've kept the faith with my country. I volunteered for the Army. I served in Vietnam. I kept the faith with my family. Tipper and I have been married for 30 years. We have devoted ourselves to our children. I have kept the faith with our country. Nine times I have raised my hand to take an oath to the Constitution, and I have never violated that oath."

—presidential debate in St. Louis, October 17, 2000

"I think the purpose of life is to glorify God. I turn to my faith as the bedrock of my approach to any important questions in my life."

—New York Times, May 29, 1999

"Everything in the Bible makes sense to me. I interpret it my own way, and that's what my tradition teaches me to do. There are poetic passages that speak eloquently to me with meanings that transcend the literal words. I want people to see my [religious] experience as what it is, the most important thing in my life."

—*New York Times,* October 22, 2000

"It certainly did not escape me that there was considerable irony in my presiding over my own defeat in the counting of the electoral votes [in the U.S. Senate]. But that irony couldn't hold a candle to the honor of discharging the constitutional duty."

—*Washington Post,* November 17, 2002

"I didn't have to stay quiet [about the 2000 election]. I could have handled the whole thing differently, and instead of making a concession speech, launched a four-year rear guard guerrilla campaign to undermine the legitimacy of the Bush presidency, and to mobilize for a rematch. And there was no shortage of advice to do that. I don't know—I felt like maybe 150 years ago, in Andrew Jackson's time, or however many years ago that is, that might have been feasible. But in the 21st century, with America the acknowledged leader of the world community, there's so much riding on the success of any American president and taking the reins of power and holding them firmly, I just didn't feel like it was in the best interest of the United States, or that it was a responsible course of action. I don't think I made the wrong decision, but I could certainly—if somebody hired me as a lawyer to write a brief on the other side, I wouldn't have any trouble doing it."

—*Washington Post,* November 17, 2002

"I thoroughly love public policy because it is a way to make life better for people who can't do it alone. I grew up in two places: in Carthage, Tennessee, and Washington, D.C. And when I was growing up I saw the gap that opened up between my friends who were from well-to-do families in Washington and my friends who were from not so well-to-do families in Tennessee. And my friends in Tennessee were just as bright, and had just as much potential, but ended up with much less opportunity because the educational system and the economy did not allow them as much of a chance to develop their potential. I think that's wrong. I think the future of the United States, whether you're in high technology or an older industry, depends on our ability to develop the talents of all our people."

—*Red Herring,* October 30, 2000

Q: Do you want your daughter Karenna to go into politics?
A: I want her to do what she wants to do. I think her judgment is so good, and if she were to decide to go into politics, she would be so good. If I had half of the skills that she has, I would definitely be in my second term as president right now.

—*GQ*, December 2006

"If I do my job right, all the candidates will be talking about the climate crisis. And I'm not convinced the presidency is the highest and best role I could play. The path I see is a path that builds a consensus—to the point where it doesn't matter as much who's running. It would take a lot to disabuse me of the notion that my highest and best use is to keep building that consensus."

—*Time*, May 16, 2007

Q: After 2000 was there a temptation for you to keep away from public life?
A: Sure, yeah. And I could easily have made that choice but this issue [on global warming] has felt like a mission to me. And I know that word is a tricky one to use. But I'm not comfortable when I'm not trying to deliver this message. If you were walking along the beach by yourself and a bottle washed up with a cork and inside was a note in it saying, "urgent—life or death, please deliver this message to the following address," you

would feel, because of the circumstances, a moral obligation to deliver the message. It's been that way for me the last 30 years. I expected the message would be heard and understood and delivered by lots of other people and the system would have long now begun to respond effectively, but none of that happened. And yet here that message remains in my hand undelivered, or at least not received, and [*Inconvenient Truth*] makes it possible to deliver that message to more people.

—IndieLondon.com, May 2006

"I've found other ways to serve my country and I enjoy them. When I'm giving my slide show, I see looks of recognition in the audience, and I hear afterwards how people are changing their lives because of the slide show or the movie. I'm fulfilled by that. And I also feel good that I think I'm making progress."

—*Der Spiegel* (Germany), July 21, 2006

"I honestly believe that the role I can most usefully play is to change the minds of the American people."

"I'm involved in a campaign, but it's not a campaign for a candidacy, it's a campaign for a cause. And the cause is to change the minds of people all over the world, especially in the U.S., about why we have to solve the climate crisis. If we don't do that, the rest of it doesn't matter at all. It won't matter how you are remembered in the history books if there are no history books. And no one to read them!"

—*Der Spiegel* (Germany), July 21, 2006

HOLLYWOOD

"Hollywood isn't very different from Washington, D.C. [Both] seem to have a lot of outsized personalities. Maybe that's why I'm attracted to both."

—*Entertainment Weekly,* July 13, 2006

"My fellow Americans, people all over the world, we need to solve the climate crisis. It's not a political issue, it's a moral issue. We have everything we need to get started, with the possible exception of the will to act. That's a renewable resource, let's renew it."

—Academy Awards acceptance speech for best documentary,
February 27, 2007

"*[An Inconvenient Truth]* is Davis Guggenheim's movie. As the director, he shaped it and provided the creative vision for how the different elements would be pieced together. Now, that said, the core of it is the slide show. It was a collaborative process but the important creative judgments were all his."

—*The Stranger* (Seattle), June 1, 2006

"Audiences don't see *[An Inconvenient Truth]* as political. Paramount did a number of focus-group screenings, and that was very clear."

—*New York* Magazine, May 22, 2006

"I have had other offers. But, frankly, Jay, when you refuse to do nude scenes, it really cuts down on the opportunities. I just want to clarify. I have no plans to do a nude scene. I have no intention to do a nude scene. I don't expect to do a nude scene."

—*The Tonight Show with Jay Leno,* June 8, 2006

Jay Leno: How do you feel being treated like a movie star?

Gore: Well, it's not all that easy. For example, I'm in this huge feud with Lindsay Lohan now.

Leno: Really? Can you give us a little more?

Gore: No, she knows what she did.

—*The Tonight Show with Jay Leno,* June 8, 2006

"Lawrence Bender, who made all of Quentin Tarantino's movies, produced [*An Inconvenient Truth*] and the production schedule was so grueling, I told him he ought to call this one *Kill Al, Vol. 1.*"

—on filming *An Inconvenient Truth*

"I'll be twice as cool as that president guy in the *West Wing.*"

—from the "Top 10" rejected Gore-Lieberman campaign slogans, as presented by Al Gore on *The Late Show with David Letterman,* September 14, 2000

"I think I may have a future as a disembodied head."
—referring to his appearance on *Futurama*,
The Associated Press, November 8, 2002

"I actually just performed a voice-over role in a movie last week. I am reprising my role as a disembodied head in *Futurama*, which is being made into a movie. There are a significant number of people who appear not to know or care that I was Vice President of the United States, but who are very tuned into the fact that I uttered the immortal line, 'I have ridden the mighty moonworm.'"
—GQ, December 2006

"[*An Inconvenient Truth's*] director, Davis Guggenheim, said that one of the huge differences between a live stage performance and a movie is that when you're in the same room with a live person who's on stage speaking—even if it's me—there's an element of dramatic tension and human connection that keeps your attention."
—Grist.org, May 9, 2006

"The purpose of a trailer is very different from the purpose of a movie. I talked with Steven Spielberg, who saw [*An Inconvenient Truth*] and loved it, and saw the trailer and loved it. He said, 'Al, you've got to know this: the purpose of a trailer is to grab an audience by the throat and wrestle them into the seat. They've got two minutes instead of 92 minutes, and they want to get people in to see the movie.'"

—Grist.org, May 9, 2006

"That word—star—it hits my ear with a little too much irony. Rin Tin Tin was a movie star. Not me."

—*Entertainment Weekly,* July 13, 2006

Q: So, did you ever think your movie would be this successful?
A: No! You know, I hoped it would be. But I had questions about whether it would really be possible to turn a slide show into a movie.

—GQ, December 2006

TECHNOLOGY

"This afternoon, I want to talk to you about the new economy and the limited but critical role that I think government should play in the twenty-first century. So here goes: Gore on the New Economy—Version 1.0. You'll be notified about upgrades."
—speech at the Microsoft CEO Summit, Seattle, May 8, 1997

"I genuinely believe that the creation of this nationwide [computer] network will create an environment where work stations are common in homes and even small businesses."
—as chairman of the Senate Science Subcommittee, 1989

"During my service in the United States Congress, I took the initiative in creating the Internet."
—speaking to Wolf Blitzer on CNN, March 9, 1999

Q: What is the biggest mistake you have made in your political career?

A: I would say that my biggest mistake was in my choice of words when I claimed to have taken the lead in the Congress in creating the Internet. I'm proud of what I did in that area, incidentally, because there was a little network called DARPANET in the Pentagon, and I did take the lead in the Congress in providing funding for the people who created what later became the Internet.

—Democratic presidential primary debate at Dartmouth College, New Hampshire, October 28, 1999

"In my first term in Congress—I was elected in 1976—I began a series of meetings, under the rubric of a group called the Congressional Clearinghouse on the Future, between interested members of Congress and company scientists, geneticists, futurists, and others. It became apparent that the juice was in the information revolution. This had particular significance for me, because when I was ten, my father who was the author of the Interstate Highway Bill, often took me to the meetings that designed the interstate-highway system. Years later, that analogy jumped out of me. Just as the proliferation of cars and trucks after World War II made the two-lane roads obsolete, the proliferation of personal computers and the growth of processing power—in the wake of the Apollo program—made the old two-lane information pathways obsolete."

—*Rolling Stone,* November 9, 2000

"Remember, America, I gave you the Internet and I can take it away."

> —from "Top 10 Rejected Gore-Lieberman 2000 Campaign Slogans," read by Al Gore on the *Late Show with David Letterman,* September 14, 2000

"The print revolution—or, as Marshall McLuhan called it, 'the Gutenberg Galaxy'—distributed an enormous amount of civic information widely throughout national language groups and helped to focus the definition of the nation-state. And over two or three centuries it empowered enough people with enough information to make possible the version of democracy that accompanied at first the U.S. revolution, and then less successfully the French revolution. Now, computer networks multiply by many fold the amount of information available to the average citizen, thereby empowering the average citizen to play a larger role still."

> —*Red Herring,* October 30, 2000

"We should keep the moratorium on taxing transactions on the Internet while the questions are dealt with."

> —Democratic presidential debate in Los Angeles, March 1, 2000

"A few decades ago, IBM predicted that the total market worldwide for computers would be a few dozen."
—speaking to Wolf Blitzer on CNN, March 9, 1999

"Today, in the Information Age, connecting all our people to a universe of knowledge and learning is the key to ensuring a lifetime of success. The facts are clear—and startling. Five years ago, three million people were connected to the Internet. Two years ago, forty million people were connected. Last year, it was one hundred million. No one knows where we will be next year, but the course is clear; technology is transforming our lives. Today, we can order blue jeans and cars custom-made to our specifications. Small businesses spring up overnight and provide services to millions. Schools are using the Internet to explore the Red Planet, dissect virtual frogs, and learn foreign languages. The Information Age is all around us—and it's here to stay."
—speech at Digital Divide Event, April 28, 1998

"Last month, in Russia, I had a chance to see close up a country that tried to hold back the Information Age—a country that used to put armed guards in front of copiers. In a way, we should be grateful it did; that helped strengthen the desire of Russian people to end communism."
—speech at UCLA, Los Angeles, California, January 11, 1994

"Go farther back to Nathaniel Hawthorne, 150 years ago: 'The world is a great vibrating brain.' What we're witnessing now [with networked computers] is a process of dynamic change that's faster and more powerful than anything in the history of humankind."

—*Red Herring*, October 30, 2000

"Competition is in the best interest of the business community. I consider myself extremely pro-business. I cast my lot with the entrepreneurs, with the small business operators, with the up-and-coming companies that are breaking into the big time on the sheer guts and energy that their innovators have shown."

—*Red Herring*, October 30, 2000

"The power of government should not be locked away in Washington, but put at your services—no further away than your keyboard. [I want government] online—so you don't have to stand in line."

—*New York Times*, June 5, 2000

"Some say we should take no action at all—just let children roam free on the Internet. To them I say: children are not miniature adults. They are vulnerable and impressionable, and we have an obligation to protect them from harmful words and images on the Internet."

—speech at the National PTA Legislative Conference, March 23, 1998

"It's a debate about a twenty-first century question: how do we keep our children safe while protecting the First Amendment and preserving the limitless opportunities of this exciting new technological medium that changes form and content on a daily basis? Blocking your own child's access to objectionable Internet content is not censoring; that's called parenting. And it's essential."

—speech on Focus on Children, an Internet summit, Washington, D.C., December 2, 1997

"A lot of parents do not know that the Internet, for all of its great wonders and riches, has some dark alleyways that are red-light districts and free-fire zones."

—CNN *Larry King Live*, May 6, 1999

"The telecommunications bills pending before the Congress, and especially the House bill, represent a contract with 100 companies. The highest bidders, not the highest principles, have set the bar. America's technological future is under attack by shortsighted ideologues, who pretend to understand history, but in fact have no understanding whatsoever."

—*Wired*, December. 1995

"President Clinton doesn't use e-mail very much now, but he plans to start. One of the driving forces that will push him to get on the computer on a regular basis is the fact that Chelsea is going to college in California. I've told him of the joys of communicating with your children off at college by way of e-mail."

—*Washington Post*, November 29, 1997

"As we gather today to talk about technology and the future, I want to share with you a list I found not long ago in an airline magazine of thirty-one signs that technology has taken over your life. According to the list, you know technology has taken over your life: If you know your email address, but not your telephone number; if you rotate your computer screen saver more than your tires; if you have never sat through a movie without having at least one electronic device on your body beep or buzz; and my personal favorite, number 23—if Al Gore strikes you as an 'intriguing fellow.'"

—speech at the International Telecommunications Union,
Minneapolis, Minnesota, October 12, 1998

"We must remember that—especially in this global economy and Information Age—we are all connected, from Minnesota to Mongolia, from Madrid to Mali. That is a vision that was not even imaginable back in 1947, when the International Telecommunication Union last met in the United States. That year, two scientists working at Bell Labs—John Bardeen and Walter Brattain—made an amazing discovery. Using a little slab of germanium, a thin plastic wedge, a shiny strip of gold foil, and a make-shift spring fashioned from an old paper clip, they were able to boost an electrical signal by more than 450 times. They called their invention a transistor. There are now more than half a billion transistors manufactured every second. Every hour, more than a trillion of them are packed into everything from computers to car engines, satellite systems to gas pumps. Within two years, a single microchip will routinely contain one billion transistors—and the patterns etched on them will be as complicated as a roadmap of the entire planet. Fifty years ago, it cost $5 for every transistor. Today, it costs 1/100th of a cent. In just a few years, it will cost a billionth of a cent."

—speech at the International Telecommunications
Union, Minneapolis, Minnesota,
October 12, 1998

"I once used the old cliché with a college audience that if the automobile had made the same exponential advances as the transistor, a car would get 100,000 miles to the gallon and cost only 50 cents. And then one of the students in the first row said, 'Sure, Mr. Vice President, but it would be less than a millimeter long.'"

> —speech at the International Telecommunications Union, Minneapolis, Minnesota, October 12, 1998

"Four years ago, I set forth five principles that I believe are essential to reap the full harvest of the Global Information Infrastructure. Those five principles were: private investment, competition, open access, flexible regulatory framework, and universal service."

> —speech at the International Telecommunications Union, Minneapolis, Minnesota, October 12, 1998

"Right now, 65 percent of the world's households have no phone service. Half of the world's population has never made a phone call. Iceland has more Internet hosts than all of Africa. Today, I challenge the business community to create a global business plan—to put data and voice telecommunication within an hour's walk of everybody on the planet by the end of the next decade."

> —speech at the International Telecommunications Union, Minneapolis, Minnesota, October 12, 1998

"Just by knowing your Social Security number, a thief is able to steal your identity and your money. I will make it a national priority to stop this kind of traffic in personal data. I'll start by making it a federal crime to buy or sell anyone's Social Security number. Let's put the 'security' back in Social Security. Together, we have to send a clear message to all our people—no matter how our technology grows and changes, your fundamental right to privacy is something that must never change."

—statement to reporters, June 8, 2000

"We first used sand in an hourglass to measure time. Now we use it to form the silicon chip that powers personal computers. Same object, more creative use."
—speech at the Microsoft CEO Summit, Seattle, May 8, 1997

"At a time when there is more computer power in a Palm Pilot than in the spaceship that took Neil Armstrong to the moon, we will offer all our people lifelong learning and new skills for the higher-paying jobs of the future. At a time when the amount of human knowledge is doubling every five years, and science and technology are advancing so rapidly, we will do bold things to make our schools the best in the world. I will fight for the greatest single commitment to education since the G.I. Bill."
—acceptance speech at the Democratic National
Convention, August 16, 2000

"You'll thank us in four years when the escalator to the moon is finished."
—from the "Top 10" rejected Gore-Lieberman 2000 campaign slogans, as presented by Al Gore on *The Late Show with David Letterman*, September 14, 2000

"Broadband interconnection is supporting decentralized processes that reinvigorate democracy. We can see it happening before out eyes. As a society we are getting smarter. Network democracy is taking hold. You can feel it."
—*The New Republic* online, June 13, 2007

"Private sector innovation can help us stop global warming-without economic cooling."
—speech at Economic Club of Detroit, May 8, 1998

"When we introduce the right incentives for eliminating pollution and becoming more efficient, many businesses will begin to make greater use of computers and advanced monitoring systems to identify even more opportunities for savings. This is what happened in the computer chip industry when more powerful chips led to better computers, which in turn made it possible to design even more powerful chips, in a virtuous cycle of steady improvement that became known as 'Moore's Law.' We may well see the emergence of a new version of 'Moore's Law' producing steadily higher levels of energy efficiency at steadily lower cost."

—speech at New York University School of Law,
New York City, September 18, 2006

"When the Internet was invented—and I assure you I intend to choose my words carefully here—it was because defense planners in the Pentagon forty years ago were searching for a way to protect America's command and communication infrastructure from being disrupted in a nuclear attack. The network they created—known as ARPANET—was based on 'distributed communication' that allowed it to continue functioning even if part of it was destroyed. Today, our nation faces threats very different from those we countered during the Cold War. We worry today that terrorists might try to inflict great damage on America's energy infrastructure by attacking a single vulnerable part of the oil distribution or electricity distribution network. So, taking a page from the early pioneers of ARPANET, we should develop a distributed electricity and liquid fuels distribution network that is less dependent on large coal-fired generating plants and vulnerable oil ports and refineries. Small windmills and photovoltaic solar cells distributed widely throughout the electricity grid would sharply reduce CO_2 emissions and at the same time increase our energy security."

—speech at New York University School of Law, New York City, September 18, 2006

"Just as a robust information economy was triggered by the introduction of the Internet, a dynamic new renewable energy economy can be stimulated by the development of an 'electranet,' or smart grid, that allows individual homeowners and business—owners anywhere in America to use their own renewable sources of energy to sell electricity into the grid when they have a surplus and purchase it from the grid when they don't. The same electranet could give homeowners and business-owners accurate and powerful tools with which to precisely measure how much energy they are using where and when, and identify opportunities for eliminating unnecessary costs and wasteful usage patterns."

—speech at New York University School of Law, New York City, September 18, 2006

"I doubt nuclear power will play a much larger role than it does now. There are serious problems that have to be solved, and they are not limited to the long-term waste-storage issue and the vulnerability-to-terrorist-attack issue. If we ever got to the point where we wanted to use nuclear reactors to back out a lot of coal, it would increase the risk of weapons-grade material being available."

—Grist.org, May 9, 2006

"We're not far off from a new generation of fuel cells that can also burn cellulosic ethanol, so you can grow your own electricity. If it's material like switchgrass and sawgrass [native North American crops], you can have no-till agriculture without the chemically intensive techniques that are used commonly for corn and wheat now. Corn may play a role in this, but it's not the way to go."

—*The Stranger* (Seattle), June 1, 2006

"The old cliché about six months being a lifetime in politics is probably out of date now with the new technology coming wave upon wave."

—*Newsweek*, April 28, 2006

"Most of us feel we have a lot more information than we can possibly deal with. A friend of mine in the computer industry once made this point by saying that if you described our human brains in computer terms, you'd have to say we have a low bit-rate but high resolution. We do, however, have very high resolution, which means we can quickly absorb the meaning of patterns containing huge quantities of data at a single gulp, and infer the meaning of each bit by reference to its context. There are two hundred billion stars in the Milky Way. We recognize the pattern instantly. Bill and Melinda [Gates'] daughter, Jennifer, recognized their faces within two weeks of her birth—a task no computer can yet replicate with speed or accuracy."

—speech at the Microsoft CEO Summit, Seattle, May 8, 1997

"As recently as 1987, AT&T was still projecting that it would take until the year 2010 to convert 95 percent of its long distance network to digital technology. Then it became pressed by the competition. The result? AT&T made its network virtually 100 percent digital by the end of 1991. Meanwhile, over the last decade the price of interstate long distance service for the average residential customer declined over 50 percent."

—speech at UCLA, Los Angeles, California,
January 11, 1994

"The heroes of Chernobyl did not die so that we would remain in ignorance. Their deaths must be turned into lessons of great beauty and hope. The truth taught by Chernobyl is that we are all connected—forever. We can choose to learn how to care for one another and the earth in a way that is worthy at last of our children's innocent trust in us; or we can choose once again, as we have so bitterly over the course of the last millennium, to persevere in our old habits of destruction and fail their trust. The challenge of Chernobyl is to recognize that the circumference of our responsibility has become the earth itself. Maybe, just maybe, the dangers of our newest technology will move us back to the safety of our oldest wisdom—the wisdom of kindness. Humankind has never fully practiced this wisdom before. But survival has not demanded it before, and it does now. This is, as historians say, an 'open moment'—a tremendous moment of choice that every nation can seize— not merely to survive, but to grow and thrive."
—speech at Chernobyl Museum, Kiev, Russia, July 23, 1998

"In the whirlwind of the bio-revolution, we must hold tight to our deepest and oldest values, and make them one with our newest science. In particular, we cannot let our newest discoveries serve as the newest excuse to unleash the vulnerability to discrimination that has plagued us throughout human history—on the basis of race and ethnicity, religion and gender, and now, genetic predisposition to disease. Modern genetics offers some of the most irrefutable arguments for the commonality of humankind. For example, scientists tell us that the differences between people of one race and people of another race are slight indeed. We share 99.9% of the estimated three billion bits of genetic information encoded in our DNA. In fact, there can be more genetic difference within racial groups than between them; a black person and a white person could be closer in their genetic make-up than two blacks or two whites."

—James D. Watson Lecture, at the National Academy of Sciences, Washington, D.C., January 20, 1998

"We all know about the double-helix. And we've all heard of the double-edged sword. Welcome to the world of the double-edged helix. As many of you know, this is a gene chip—a thin slice of silicon about the size of a postage stamp that promises to have an enormous impact on the future of medicine. On one hand, it will give us critical information about our genetic codes. On the other hand, it will test our ability as a people to deal with the ramifications of that information. Within a decade, it will be possible for our doctor[s] to take a cheek swab, place a few of our cells on a gene chip scanner, and quickly analyze our genetic predisposition to scores of diseases."

—James D. Watson Lecture, at the National Academy of Sciences, Washington, D.C., January 20, 1998

"Today, the fear of genetic discrimination is prompting Americans to avoid genetic tests that could literally save their lives. And that can make this form of discrimination a serious threat to our public health. According to one study, 63% of Americans would not take a genetic test if their health insurers or employers could get access to the results. Many women have put off getting genetic tests for breast cancer because of a fear of discrimination."

—James D. Watson Lecture, at the National Academy of Sciences, Washington, D.C., January 20, 1998

"How did the electronic communication revolution begin? Samuel Morse was a portrait painter. In fact, his painting of James Monroe hangs in the White House today. While Morse was working on a portrait of General Lafayette in Washington, his wife—who lived about 300 miles away—grew ill and died. But it took seven days for the news to reach him. In his grief and remorse, he began to wonder whether it was possible to erase barriers of time and space—so no one would be unable to reach a loved one in time of need. Pursuing this thought, he came to discover how to use electricity to convey messages—and so he invented the telegraph. Emotion led to innovation."

—speech at the Microsoft CEO Summit, Seattle, May 8, 1997

"Larry [Page] and Sergey [Brin] and the entire executive team had false beards on."

—referring to his first day at Google, Fast Company,
July/August 2007

"And just as the information revolution was based on the more precise tracking and channeling of bits of data, our whole economy is on the verge of becoming much more granular in the precision with which it tracks atoms and molecules and electrons and protons. How is it that we waste 90% of the energy that we think we're using? It's crazy. But that's the reality today. And as we eliminate that waste, we save money that can be used more rationally for other things. I think of it as having two waves. The first wave is made up of all the technologies that we presently have available: hybrids, conservation efficiency, carbon capture and sequestration. But the second wave involves the new and more advanced technologies that are ten or twelve years away but with increased and accelerated R&D can be five to seven years away: nano-manufacturing, positional manufacturing technologies that use carbon fiber and these new cutting-edge materials that don't require the massive energy for processing ore and digging into the ground and generating these huge waste strains, but rather, the very precise use, molecule by molecule, of exactly what's needed for what purpose."

—The Stranger (Seattle), June 1, 2006

"We had this meeting in London for Generation [an investment fund] and there was a presentation that looks at all the business ideas that can be invested in. There're ideas that are mature, ideas that are maturing, ideas that are past their prime, venture-capital-stage ideas—and a category called 'predawn.' And all of a sudden it hit me: Most of my political career was spent investing in predawn ideas! I thought, 'Oh, that's where I went wrong!'"

—*New York*, May 22, 2006

"Please don't recount this vote."
—Webby Lifetime Achievement Award acceptance speech (limited to five words), June 6, 2005

THE MEDIA

"It is possible to speculate that a 'role requirement' of the President in the future might become 'visual communication.'"
—from Al Gore's Harvard senior thesis, "The Impact of Television on the Conduct of the Presidency, 1947–1969"

"All the stories about reinvention, about me changing my image, trying to be something I'm not—all of those were superficial manifestations of the deeper perception of many in the press corps."
—*Rolling Stone,* November 9, 2000

"[The system] is like a washing machine that is permanently set on the spin cycle. It doesn't stop spinning. That creates real problems for a politics based on reason."
—*The Tennessean,* June 2, 2007

"The media is kind of weird these days on politics, and there are some major institutional voices that are, truthfully speaking, part and parcel of the Republican Party. Fox News Network, *The Washington Times*, Rush Limbaugh—there's a bunch of them, and some of them are financed by wealthy ultra-conservative billionaires who make political deals with Republican administrations and the rest of the media."

—*Time,* June 18, 2003

"The [Bush] Administration works closely with a network of 'rapid response' digital Brown Shirts who work to pressure reporters and their editors."

—American Constitution Society speech, Georgetown University Law Center, Washington, D.C., June 24, 2004

"There was never a golden age when everything was all logical. But the relative role of facts and logic and reason used to be much larger than it has become in the age of 30-second TV ads and the multi-screen experience."

—*Countdown with Keith Olbermann,* May 29, 2007

"Television news programs have probably spent a lot more time on Britney Spears shaving her head, and Paris Hilton going to jail, and Anna-Nicole Smith's estate lawyers, and Joey Buttafuoco, and all this stuff, than they have spent giving us the facts—for example, telling us before the invasion of Iraq, that actually Iraq had nothing whatsoever to do with the attack of 9/11."

—*The Daily Show with Jon Stewart*, May 25, 2007

"Clearly, the purpose of television news is no longer to inform the American people or serve the public interest. It is to 'glue eyeballs to the screen' in order to build ratings and sell advertising. And more importantly, notice what is not on: the global climate crisis, the nation's fiscal catastrophe, the hollowing out of America's industrial base, and a long list of other serious public questions that need to be addressed by the American people. One morning not long ago, I flipped on one of the news programs in hopes of seeing information about an important world event that had happened earlier that day. But the lead story was about a young man who had been hiccupping for three years. And I must say, it was interesting; he had trouble getting dates. But what I didn't see was news."

—speech at the American Press Institute, Reston, Virginia, October 5, 2005

"We need to open up the medium of television to the participation of individuals, and reestablish respect for truth. Because when we ignore it, that's what invites problems. M. Scott Peck, who, among other things, wrote that fabulous book, *The Road Less Traveled* had a unique and interesting definition of the word 'evil.' He said, 'Evil is absence of truth.' If we have a system that makes people comfortable in ignoring the truth, they're not curious about the truth, then the preconceived notions driven by ideology or power politics or special interests are going to determine the outcome of any reasoned debate."

—*Charlie Rose*, May 25, 2007

"The system forces [presidential candidates] to concentrate on these impressionistic approaches that come out of the daily news cycle and the tit-for-tat of what is a hot buzzword issue of the day. And they also have to deal with the media's obsession with the so-called horse race."

—*CNN Larry King Live*, May 22, 2007

"In the run-up to the Iraq War, a lot of politicians, but also a lot of newscasters, were actually *scared* that they would be branded as unpatriotic, or lose access, or lose ratings. Some of the businesses that advise television networks on how to build

their ratings, advised them point-blank, *do not* put on opponents to this invasion of Iraq, because the others are waving the flag and saying, 'Let's go.'"
—*The Daily Show with Jon Stewart,* May 25, 2007

"A few loud voices have enough money to buy repetitive messages, like the ExxonMobil ads on the op-ed page of *The New York Times.* As the big money fueling political commercials does these little short slogans, it becomes even more difficult for a self-governing democracy to be honest with itself."
—*Rolling Stone,* July 13–27, 2006

"The leadership of the Republican party is augmented by its links to the corporate ownership of the conglomerates that control most of our media. And this, after all, includes a growing part of the media characterized by paranoia presented as entertainment—the part that allows drug-addled hypocrites, compulsive gamblers, and assorted religious bigots to masquerade as moral guides for the nation."
—speech at the New School, New York City, February 4, 2004

"The movie *Network,* which won the Best Picture Oscar in 1976, was presented as a farce but was actually a prophecy. The journalism profession morphed into the news business, which became the media industry and is now completely owned by conglomerates. The news divisions—which used to be seen as serving a public interest and were subsidized by the rest of the network—are now seen as profit centers designed to generate revenue and, more importantly, to advance the larger agenda of the corporation of which they are a small part. They have fewer reporters, fewer stories, smaller budgets, less travel, fewer bureaus, less independent judgment, more vulnerability to influence by management, and more dependence on government sources and canned public relations hand-outs."

—speech at the American Press Institute,
Reston, Virginia, October 5, 2005

"In the world of television, the massive flows of information are largely in only one direction, which makes it virtually impossible for individuals to take part in what passes for a national conversation. Individuals receive, but they cannot send. They hear, but they do not speak. The 'well-informed citizenry' is in danger of becoming the 'well-amused audience.'"

—from Al Gore's *The Assault on Reason*

"The U.S. Press was recently found in a comprehensive inter-national study to be only the twenty-seventh freest press in the world. And that too seems strange to me. Among the other fac-tors damaging our public discourse in the media, the imposi-tion by management of entertainment values on the journalism profession has resulted in scandals, fabricated sources, fictional events, and the tabloidization of mainstream news."

—speech at the American Press Institute,
Reston, Virginia, October 5, 2005

"I do go to Drudge from time to time."

—Politico.com, May 31, 2007

"When I go to a site that I know is more likely than not to agree with my point of view, I will quite often go laterally to the opposite side of the court to see what's being said."

—Politico.com, May 31, 2007

"Even with the rise of the Internet and its growing strength, television is now so dominant that, just to take one example, in the last elections in the contested races candidates in both parties spent an average of 80% of their campaign budget not on the Internet or on pamphlets or newspaper or magazine ads but on thirty-second TV ads. That's what works now, and the way it works is troubling. It's not a multi-way conversation. It's not even a two-way conversation."

—*The New Republic* online, June 13, 2007

"And for all of its excesses and bad features, the Internet does invite a robust multi-way conversation that I think is already beginning to serve as a corrective for some of the abuses of the mass media persuasion campaigns that brought us the invasion of Iraq and the ignoring of the climate crisis and the other serious mistakes that we've been making over the last few years."

—*Countdown with Keith Olbermann*, May 29, 2007

"The more important question is how the United States of America could have been so vulnerable to such crass manipulation (about going to war in Iraq]. Many were afraid of being branded unpatriotic, sure, and many journalists were, as many have since acknowledged, and that is unhealthy in a democracy."

—*The Guardian* (UK), June 2, 2007

"I do believe that the Internet has brought about a continuing and accelerating revolution in the technique of politics and the way candidates reach out to connect with individual voters and groups. But where the wholesale messaging is concerned, television is still completely dominant. It's quasi-hypnotic. One of the most valuable things in the television business if you're a content creator is to have a good lead-in show before you. Why? Not only do [viewers] not get up—a significant percentage are incapable of moving a thumb muscle to hit the remote because there's a quasi-trance that sets in. I don't want to over-dramatize it, but the fact is that people just sit there entranced—and that's why most of the money in politics goes to television."

—*Newsweek*, April 28, 2006

"At first I thought the exhaustive, non-stop coverage of the O.J. trial was just an unfortunate excess that marked an unwelcome departure from the normal good sense and judgment of our television news media. But now we know that it was merely an early example of a new pattern of serial obsessions that periodically take over the airwaves for weeks at a time."

—speech at the American Press Institute,
Reston, Virginia, October 5, 2005

"What I do think is interesting is that some of the comedy news programs are so frequently more successful than the established news programs in presenting some of the more provocative—dare I say inconvenient—truths that emerge from the daily narrative of American democracy. Just as the court jester was sometimes the only truthsayer who could avoid having his head off in medieval feudal courts, a similar phenomenon appears to have emerged in our culture."

—Politico.com, May 31, 2007

"There is a difference between scientific uncertainty and political uncertainty. Where science thrives on the unknown, politics is often paralyzed by it. Yet the dialogue between science and politics has not yet accounted for this difference. In this case, when 98 percent of the scientists in a given field share one view and two percent disagree, both viewpoints are sometimes presented in a format [by the news media] in which each appears equally credible."

—from Al Gore's *Earth in the Balance*

"Politicians often confuse self-interested arguments paid for by lobbyists and planted in the popular press with legitimate peer-reviewed studies published in reputable scientific journals. For example, the global warming skeptics cite one article more than

any other in arguing that global warming is just a myth: a statement of concern during the 1970s that the world might be in
danger of entering a new ice age. But that article was published
in *Newsweek* and never appeared in a peer-reviewed journal."

—from *An Inconvenient Truth* (book)

"Whenever a chief executive spends prodigious amounts of
energy convincing people of lies, he damages the fabric of
democracy, and the belief in the fundamental integrity of our
self-government. That creates a need for control over the flood
of bad news, bad policies, and bad decisions."

—speech to the American Constitution Society, Georgetown
University Law Center, Washington, D.C., June 24, 2004

"As a general rule, where news is concerned, if you are the
President you have a traveling press corps, and if you are the
Party's nominee you do, too. But with those two exceptions, outside of the Scott Peterson [murder] trial, nothing—a speech, a
proposal, something in the democratic discourse—nothing will
be national news unless it occurs within a ten-minute cab ride
of downtown Manhattan or downtown Washington, D.C."

—*New Yorker*, September 13, 2004

"Television first overtook newsprint to become the dominant source of information in America in 1963. But for the next two decades, the television networks mimicked the nation's leading newspapers by faithfully following the standards of the journalism profession. And then one day, a smart young political consultant turned to an older elected official and succinctly described a new reality in America's public discourse: 'If it's not on television, it doesn't exist.' But some extremely important elements of American Democracy have been pushed to the sidelines. And the most prominent casualty has been the 'marketplace of ideas' that was so beloved and so carefully protected by our Founders. It effectively no longer exists."

—speech at the American Press Institute,
Reston, Virginia, October 5, 2005

"The coverage of political campaigns focuses on the 'horse race' and little else. And the well-known axiom that guides most local television news is 'if it bleeds, it leads.' To which some disheartened journalists add, 'If it thinks, it stinks.'"

—speech at the American Press Institute,
Reston, Virginia, October 5, 2005

THE ACCIDENTAL PRESIDENT: GEORGE W. BUSH'S REIGN OF LIES, TERROR, AND FEAR

"In many ways, George W. Bush reminds me more of Nixon than any other previous president. Like Bush, Nixon subordinated virtually every principal to his hunger for reelection. After he was driven from office in disgrace, one of Nixon's confidants quoted Nixon as having told him this: 'People react to fear, not love.'"

—speech at the New School, New York City, February 4, 2004

"Bush's failures have been spectacular. The evidence of deceit, miscalculation have combined to produce in the minds of a lot of people a growing conviction that it's really not good for America."

—*New Yorker,* September 13, 2004

"I think [Bush] is a bully, and, like all bullies, he's a coward when confronted with a force that he's fearful of. His reaction to the extravagant and unbelievably selfish wish list of the wealthy interest groups that put him in the White House is obsequious. The degree of obsequiousness that is involved in saying 'yes, yes, yes, yes, yes' to whatever these people want, no matter the damage and harm done to the nation as a whole—that can come only from genuine moral cowardice. I don't see any other explanation for it, because it's not a question of principle."

—*New Yorker*, September 13, 2004

Q: What surprises you most about how the Bush presidency has turned out?

A: I guess what surprises me most is his incuriosity. When his first Secretary of the Treasury came in for their first meeting and spoke for an hour about economic policies of the new administration, he asked not a single question. When he received the briefing in August of 2001 that Osama bin Laden was planning a major attack soon, you know, on the United States, he did not ask a single question. When he was briefed several days before Hurricane Katrina hit New Orleans and the weather service people were saying it may mark a return to medieval conditions, he asked not a single question. And that same incuriosity seems to be a factor when he just accepts hook, line and sinker, the ExxonMobil view that global warming is not a problem.

—*Fresh Air with Terry Gross*, NPR, May 30, 2006

"Most of the problems President Bush has caused for this country stemmed not from his belief in God but his belief in the infallibility of the right-wing Republican ideology that exalts the interest of the wealthy, and of large corporations over and above the interests of the American people. It is love of power for its own sake that is the original sin of this presidency."
—speech at Georgetown University, Washington, D.C.,
October 18, 2004

"For well over a year, the Bush administration has used its power in the wrong way. In the election of 2000, I argued that the Bush-Cheney ticket was being bankrolled by 'a new generation of special interests, power brokers who would want nothing better than a pliant president who would bend public policy to suit their purposes and profits.' Some considered this warning 'antibusiness.' It was nothing of the sort."
—Al Gore's op-ed "Broken Promises and Political Deception," *New York Times,* August 4, 2002

"In all my years of public service I have never witnessed national political leaders as corrupt, incompetent, and subservient to powerful special interests as George Bush and the Republican Rubber Stamp Congress."
—Al Gore email to donors on behalf of the Democratic Congressional Campaign Committee, May 2006

"The [Iraq War] was the single worst strategic mistake in the history of this country."

—*CNN Larry King Live,* June 13, 2006

"The evidence available showed very clearly that we had been attacked on September 11, 2001, by Osama Bin Laden and the Al Qaeda terrorist organization. And I applauded President Bush's decision to go into Afghanistan to go after Bin Laden. I thought that was correct. I think it was a mistake, though, to pull so many of our troops off of that hunt and divert to an invasion of a country that had absolutely nothing to do with attacking us."

—*CNN Larry King Live,* June 13, 2006

"I am deeply concerned that the course of action that we are presently embarking upon with respect to Iraq has the potential to seriously damage our ability to win the war against terrorism and to weaken our ability to lead the world in this new century. The vast majority of those who sponsored, planned and implemented the cold-blooded murder of more than 3,000 Americans are still at large, still neither located nor apprehended, much less punished and neutralized. I do not believe that we should allow ourselves to be distracted from this urgent task simply because it is proving to be more difficult and lengthy than was predicted. Great nations persevere and then prevail. They do not jump from one unfinished task to another. We should remain focused on the war against terrorism."

—speech at the Commonwealth Club, San Francisco,
September 23, 2002

"When the president and his team were confidently asserting that Saddam Hussein had aluminum tubes that had been acquired in order to enrich uranium for atomic bombs, numerous experts at the Department of Energy and elsewhere in the intelligence community were certain that the information being presented to our country by the president was completely wrong. The true experts on uranium enrichment are at Oak Ridge, where most enrichment has taken place in the U.S., in my home state of Tennessee. They told me early on that in their opinion there was virtually zero possibility that the tubes in question were for the purpose of enrichment. And yet they received a directive at Oak Ridge forbidding them from making any public statement that disagreed with the assertions being made to the people by President Bush."

—speech at Georgetown University, Washington, D.C.,
October 18, 2004

"The widely respected arms expert David Kay concluded a lengthy and extensive investigation in Iraq for the Bush administration with these words: 'We were all wrong.' The real meaning of Kay's devastating verdict is that for more than two years, President Bush and his administration have been distorting America's political reality by force-feeding the American people a grossly exaggerated fear of Iraq that was hugely disproportionate to the actual danger posed by Iraq."

—speech at the New School, New York City,
February 4, 2004

"I think Bush put forward a counterfeit large vision. The war in Iraq was postured as a big idea. Well, it was a big dumb idea. And, again, I don't think he's dumb, but I think that idea is dumb."

—*New Yorker*, September 13, 2004

"What the invasion of Iraq has in common with the climate crisis is that in both cases the best evidence was ignored. In both cases there was more than sufficient evidence to convince any reasonable person that the invasion of Iraq was a catastrophic mistake, and the failure to begin sharply reducing CO_2 was an even worse mistake."

—*The Guardian* (UK), June 2, 2007

"Before the vote to go to war in the first place in Iraq, our longest-serving Senator, Senator Robert Byrd of West Virginia, stood in an empty chamber, and he said 'Why is this Senate silent? Ominously silent?' There was no effort to lay out the pros and cons."

—*The Daily Show with Jon Stewart*, May 25, 2007

"[Defense] Secretary Rumsfeld, who saw all of the intelligence available to President Bush that might bear on the alleged connection between al Qaeda and Saddam Hussein, finally admitted under tough repeated questioning from reporters, and I quote, 'To my knowledge, I have not seen any strong, hard evidence that links the two,' end quote. This is not negligence. When the administration is told specifically and repeatedly that there is no linkage, and simultaneously makes bold assertions in a confident manner to the American people that leave the impression with 70 percent of the country that Saddam Hussein was primarily responsible for the attack, this is deception."

—speech at Georgetown University, Washington, D.C., October 18, 2004

"It's shocking, isn't it? Seventy percent of the American people were convinced at the time of the vote that Saddam Hussein was primarily responsible for the attack. Fifty percent *still* think he was involved with the attack."

—*The Daily Show with Jon Stewart*, May 25, 2007

"Two months before the Iraq war began, President Bush received detailed and comprehensive secret reports warning him that the likely result of an American-led invasion of Iraq would be increased support for Islamic fundamentalism, deep divisions in Iraqi society, high levels of violent internal conflict, and guerrilla warfare aimed at U.S. forces. And yet in spite of those analyses, President Bush chose to suppress those warnings, conceal that information, and instead went right on conveying to the American people the absurdly Pollyanna-ish view of highly questionable and obviously biased sources like Ahmad Chalabi, the convicted felon and known swindler, who the Bush administration put on its payroll and gave a seat adjacent to First Lady Laura Bush at the State of the Union address."

—speech at Georgetown University, Washington, D.C., October 18, 2004

"Even after the decision to invade Iraq was made, they had a preconceived notion that the best way to do it was with a very small force to go in and get it over with. And the general in charge of the United States Army, four-star General Eric Shinseki, said, 'We're going to need several hundred thousand troops for an occupation or otherwise we're inviting trouble.' And not only was he ignored, he was punished. A chilling message was sent to the rest of the military leaders, and it had a marked effect in causing them, like many of the journalists, like many of the politicians, to be quiet when their own reasoning would have led them to speak up and say, 'But! That's wrong!'"

—*Charlie Rose,* May 25, 2007

"In the early days of the unfolding catastrophe [in Iraq], the President compared our ongoing efforts in Iraq to World War II and victory over Japan. Let me cite one difference between those two historical events: When imperial Japan attacked us at Pearl Harbor, Franklin Roosevelt did not invade Indonesia."

—speech to the Sierra Summit, San Francisco,
September 9, 2005

"This war in Iraq has become a recruiting bonanza for terrorists who use it as their most damning indictment of the United States and of U.S. policy. This has been a propaganda victory for Osama bin Laden beyond his wildest dreams. And it is tragic, and it was avoidable."

—speech at Georgetown University, Washington, D.C.,
October 18, 2004

"When President Bush received his fateful and historic warning of 9/11—a CIA report that carried a headline, 'Bin Laden determined to strike in the U.S.,' [which was] more alarming and more pointed than any I saw in eight years of six-days-a-week CIA briefings—he did not convene the National Security Council, did not bring together the FBI and CIA and other agencies with responsibility to protect the nation, and apparently did not even ask follow-up questions later about the warning."

—speech at Georgetown University, Washington, D.C.,
October 18, 2004

"The fear campaign aimed at Iraq was timed for the kickoff of the midterm election campaign of 2002—you know, the one where [former Georgia Senator] Max Cleland, who lost three limbs fighting for America in Vietnam, was accused of being unpatriotic."

—speech at the New School, New York City,
February 4, 2004

"President Bush is telling us that America's most urgent requirement of the moment—right now—is not to redouble our efforts against Al Qaeda, not to stabilize the nation of Afghanistan after driving its host government from power, even as Al Qaeda members slip back across the border to set up in Afghanistan again; rather, he is telling us that our most urgent task right now is to shift our focus and concentrate on immediately launching a new war against Saddam Hussein. Now, the timing of this sudden burst of urgency to immediately take up this new cause as America's new top priority, displacing our former top priority, the war against Osama Bin Laden, was explained innocently by the White House chief of staff in his now well-known statement that 'From a marketing point of view, you don't introduce new products in August.'"
—speech at the Commonwealth Club, San Francisco,
September 23, 2002

"President George W. Bush, by contrast, is pushing for a vote in this Congress immediately before the election. That in itself is not inherently wrong, but I believe that puts a burden on the shoulders of President Bush to dispel the doubts many have expressed about the role that politics might be playing in the calculations of some in the administration. Rather than making efforts to dispel these concerns at home and abroad about the role of politics in the timing of his policy, the president is on the campaign trail two and three days a week, often publicly taunting Democrats with the political consequences of a 'no' vote. The Republican National Committee is running pre-packaged advertising based on the same theme—all of this apparently in keeping with a political strategy clearly described in a White House aide's misplaced computer disk, which advised Republican operatives that their principal game plan for success in the election a few weeks away was to 'focus on the war.'"

—speech at the Commonwealth Club, San Francisco,
September 23, 2002

"White House political advisor Karl Rove advised Republican candidates that their best political strategy was to 'run on the war.' And as soon as the troops began to mobilize, the Republican National Committee distributed yard signs throughout America saying, 'I support President Bush and the troops'—as if they were one and the same."

—speech to the American Constitution Society,
Washington, D.C., November 9, 2003

"For everything there is a season—particularly the politics of fear."

—speech at the New School, New York City,
February 4, 2004

"Our founders wouldn't be the least bit surprised at what the modern public opinion polls all tell us about why it's so important particularly for President Bush to keep the American people from discovering that what he told them about the linkage between Iraq and Al Qaeda isn't true. President Bush and Vice President Cheney have decided to fight to the rhetorical death over whether or not there's a meaningful connection between Iraq and Al Qaeda. They think that if they lose that argument and people see the truth, then they'll not only lose support for the controversial decision to go to war, but also lose some of the new power they've picked up from the Congress and the courts, and face harsh political consequences at the hands of the American people."

—speech to the American Constitution Society, Georgetown University Law Center, Washington, D.C., June 24, 2004

"Right from the start, beginning very soon after the attacks of 9/11, President Bush made a decision to start mentioning Osama bin Laden and Saddam Hussein in the same breath in a cynical mantra designed to fuse them together as one in the public's mind. He repeatedly used this device in a highly disciplined manner to create a false impression in the minds of the American people that Saddam Hussein was responsible for 9/11."

—speech to the American Constitution Society, Georgetown University Law Center, Washington, D.C., June 24, 2004

"Unlike the first Persian Gulf War, which I supported because Saddam Hussein had invaded his neighbor and was threatening the security interests of the U.S. and our allies and we had support from all our allies, the United Nations resolution, the whole world was behind us."

—*CNN Larry King Live,* June 13, 2006

"Four years ago in August of 2001, President Bush received a dire warning: 'Al Qaeda determined to attack inside the US.' No meetings were called, no alarms were sounded, no one was brought together to say, 'What else do we know about this imminent threat? What can we do to prepare our nation for what we have been warned is about to take place?' If there had been preparations, they would have found a lot of information collected by the FBI, and CIA, and NSA—including the names of most of the terrorists who flew those planes into the WTC and the Pentagon and the field in Pennsylvania. The warnings of FBI field offices that there were suspicious characters getting flight training without expressing any curiosity about the part of the training that has to do with landing. They would have found directors of FBI field offices in a state of agitation about the fact that there was no plan in place and no effective response. Instead, it was vacation time, not a time for preparation. Or protecting the American people."

—speech to the Sierra Summit, San Francisco, September 9, 2005

"You know, having spent eight years reading the intelligence briefings every morning at the start of the day, six mornings a week, and knowing what was in those reports for the final two years I was there, I was amazed to read just a few days ago that on September 11 the FBI had one agent assigned to monitor Al Qaeda and to protect us against Osama Bin Laden. I found that absolutely incredible. Well, I bite my tongue about the rest of it."

—remarks following his speech at the Commonwealth Club, San Francisco, September 23, 2002

"It is inconceivable to me that Bush would read a warning as stark and as clear as the one he received on August 6th of 2001 [about Al-Qaeda], and, according to some of the new histories, he turned to the briefer and said, 'Well, you've covered your ass.' And never called a follow up meeting. Never made an inquiry. Never asked a single question. To this day, I don't understand it. And, I think it's fair to say that he personally does in fact bear a measure of blame for not doing his job at a time when we really needed him to do his job."

—GQ, December 2006

"It's transparent to everybody that [Secretary of State] Colin Powell was marginalized. Because the right wing distrusted his values and instincts, he was made a figurehead. I like him and respect him a lot, but I think he has been (a) badly treated by this Administration and (b) allowed himself to be used in ways that have been harmful to him—more important, harmful to the country. He should have resigned, in my opinion. Absolutely. I winced quite a few times when I watched him during his presentation to the United Nations. That was a very painful experience to watch."

—*New Yorker*, September 13, 2004

"One of the hallmarks of a strategic catastrophe is that it creates a cul-de-sac from which there are no good avenues of easy departure. Taking charge of the war policy and extricating our troops as quickly as possible without making a horrible situation even worse is a little like grabbing a steering wheel in the middle of a skid."

—*New York Times* interview with op-ed columnist Bob Herbert, June 5, 2007

"Our country is suffering . . . having 150,000 of our soldiers trapped in the middle of a civil war."

—*NewsHour*, June 7, 2007

"The White House directed the formulation of legal standards that seemed to be aimed at opening up the definition of what was permissible in the treatment of captives and some of the activities that took place in the aftermath of that initiative seemed to a lay person to constitute torture. General George Washington in the American revolutionary war prohibited torture and that prohibition was kept in place through his presidency and every presidency up until the present one. Then the definitions were changed."

—*The Guardian* (UK), June 2, 2007

"Vice President Cheney was genuinely focused on trying to get a foothold in the region where the biggest oil reserves are, and he had written about and spoken about that for years before taking office."

—CNN *Larry King Live,* June 13, 2006

"There was certainly a coordinated effort in the White House and in the Department of Defense simultaneously to convey the image of a mushroom cloud exploding over an American city and to link it to a specific scenario, the very strong and explicit implication that Saddam Hussein was going to develop nuclear weapons and give them to Osama bin Laden, and that would result in nuclear explosions in American

cities. This was the principal hot-button justification for convincing the majority of people to support the invasion of
Iraq, and they selected weapons of mass destruction and the
themes related to that, not because they had the evidence to
justify it, but because it was the most effective way to manip-
ulate opinion."

—*NewsHour,* June 7, 2007

"If the [White House] genuinely believed that Saddam Hussein
was responsible for 9/11, then that's a degree of gullibility that's
quite serious. And although President Bush has since tried to
specifically distance himself from that argument, Vice President
Cheney still has not, so maybe there's a split within the administration."

—*NewsHour,* June 7, 2007

"There are some of you who would like to spend our money
on some made-up war. To you I say, 'what part of lockbox don't
you understand?'"

—as guest host on *Saturday Night Live,* May 13, 2006

"What happened at the[Abu Ghraib] prison, it is now clear, was not the result of random acts by 'a few bad apples,' it was the natural consequence of the Bush Administration policy that has dismantled those wise constraints and has made war on America's checks and balances. The abuse of the prisoners at Abu Ghraib flowed directly from the abuse of the truth that characterized the Administration's march to war and the abuse of the trust that had been placed in President Bush by the American people in the aftermath of September 11th."

—speech to MoveOn.org, New York City, May 26, 2004

"The FBI privately labeled [Dr. Martin Luther] King the 'most dangerous and effective Negro leader in the country' and vowed to 'take him off his pedestal.' The government even attempted to destroy his marriage and tried to blackmail him into committing suicide. This campaign continued until Dr. King's murder. The discovery that the FBI conducted this long-running and extensive campaign of secret electronic surveillance designed to infiltrate the inner workings of the Southern Christian Leadership Conference, and to learn the most intimate details of Dr. King's life, was instrumental in helping to convince Congress to enact restrictions on wiretapping. And yet, just one month ago, Americans awoke to the shocking news that in spite of this long settled law, the Executive Branch has been secretly spying on large numbers of Americans for the last four years. During the period when this eavesdropping was still secret, the President seemed to go out of his way to reassure the American people on more than one occasion that, of course, judicial permission is required for any government spying on American citizens and that, of course, these constitutional safeguards were still in place. But surprisingly, the President's soothing statements turned out to be false. Moreover, as soon as this massive domestic spying program was uncovered by the press, the President not only confirmed that the story was true, but in the next breath declared that he has no intention stopping or of bringing these wholesale invasions of privacy to an end."

—speech to the American Constitution Society, Washington, D.C., January 16, 2006 (MLK Day)

"An executive who arrogates to himself the power to ignore the legitimate legislative directives of the Congress or to act free of the check of the judiciary becomes the central threat that the Founders sought to nullify in the Constitution—an all-powerful executive too reminiscent of the King from whom they had broken free."

—speech to the American Constitution Society, Washington, D.C., January 16, 2006 (MLK Day)

"More than two years after they rounded up over 1,200 individuals of Arab descent, the [Justice Department] still refuse to release the names of the individuals they detained, even though virtually every one of those arrested has been 'cleared' by the FBI of any connection to terrorism and there is absolutely no national security justification for keeping the names secret. Yet at the same time, White House officials themselves leaked the name of a CIA operative serving the country, in clear violation of the law, in an effort to get at her husband, who had angered them by disclosing that the President had relied on forged evidence in his State of the Union address as part of his effort to convince the country that Saddam Hussein was on the verge of building nuclear weapons."

—speech to the American Constitution Society,
Washington, D.C., November 9, 2003

"Starting two years ago, federal agents were given broad new statutory authority by the Patriot Act to 'sneak and peak' in non-terrorism cases. They can secretly enter your home with no warning—whether you are there or not—and they can wait for months before telling you they were there. And it doesn't have to have any relationship to terrorism whatsoever. President Bush is claiming the unilateral right to do that to any American citizen he believes is an 'enemy combatant.' Those are the magic words. If the President alone decides that those two words accurately describe someone, then that person can be immediately locked up and held incommunicado for as long as the President wants, with no court having the right to determine whether the facts actually justify his imprisonment. Now if the President makes a mistake, or is given faulty information by somebody working for him, and locks up the wrong person, then it's almost impossible for that person to prove his innocence—because he can't talk to a lawyer or his family or anyone else and he doesn't even have the right to know what specific crime he is accused of committing."

—speech to the American Constitution Society,
Washington, D.C., November 9, 2003

"George W. Bush promised us a foreign policy with humility. Instead, he has brought us humiliation in the eyes of the world. He promised to 'restore honor and integrity to the White House.' Instead, he has brought deep dishonor to our country and built a durable reputation as the most dishonest President since Richard Nixon. Honor? He decided not to honor the Geneva Convention. Just as he would not honor the United Nations, international treaties, the opinions of our allies, the role of Congress and the courts. He did not honor the advice, experience, and judgment of our military leaders in designing his invasion of Iraq. And now he will not honor our fallen dead by attending any funerals or even by permitting photos of their flag-draped coffins."

—speech to MoveOn.org, New York City, May 26, 2004

"If President Bush wants to pursue honesty and integrity in the White House he should make public the names of the energy company lobbyists who advised him on energy and environmental legislation, and he should call for the release of the Securities and Exchange Commission files on the controversy surrounding his role in certain stock sales."

—Al Gore's op-ed "Broken Promises and Political Deception," *New York Times,* August 4, 2002

"The level of cynicism and crass political calculation that characterizes the Bush White House and the Republican-controlled Congress is truly breathtaking."

—Al Gore email to donors on behalf of Democratic Congressional Campaign Committee, May 2006

"The essential cruelty of Bush's game is that he takes an astonishingly selfish and greedy collection of economic and political proposals, and then cloaks them with a phony moral authority, thus misleading many Americans who have a deep and genuine desire to do good in the world. And in the process he convinces them to lend unquestioning support for proposals that actually hurt their families and their communities."

—speech at Georgetown University, Washington, D.C., October 18, 2004

"The real distinction of this Presidency is that, at its core, he is a very weak man. He projects himself as incredibly strong, but behind closed doors he is incapable of saying no to his biggest financial supporters and his coalition in the Oval Office. He's been shockingly malleable to Cheney and Rumsfeld and Wolfowitz and the whole New American Century bunch. He was rolled in the immediate aftermath of 9/11. He was too weak to resist it."

—*New Yorker,* September 13, 2004

"I'm not of the school that questions [Bush's] intelligence. There are different kinds of intelligence, and it's arrogant for a person with one kind of intelligence to question someone with another kind. He certainly is a master at some things, and he has a following. He seeks strength in simplicity. But, in today's world, that's often a problem. His weakness is a moral weakness."

—*New Yorker,* September 13, 2004

"Bush's seeming immunity to doubt is often interpreted by people who see and hear him on television as evidence of the strength of his conviction when, in fact, it is this very inflexibility based on a willful refusal to even consider alternative opinions or conflicting evidence that poses the most serious danger to our country. By the same token, the simplicity of many of his pronouncements, which are often misinterpreted as evidence that he has penetrated to the core of a complex issue, are in fact exactly the opposite because they usually mark his refusal to even consider complexity."

—speech at Georgetown University, Washington, D.C.,
October 18, 2004

"Mr. Bush took us to war on false premises and with no plan to win the peace. But more important than his record as a debater is Mr. Bush's record as a president. And therein lies the true opportunity for John Kerry—notwithstanding the president's political skills, his performance in office amounts to a catastrophic failure."

—Al Gore's op-ed "How to Debate George Bush,"
New York Times, September 29, 2004

"Baseball, our national pastime, still lies under the shadow of steroid accusations. But I have faith in Baseball Commissioner George W. Bush when he says, 'we will find the steroid users if we have to tap every phone in America.'"

—as guest host on *Saturday Night Live,* May 13, 2006

"[Bush] does what ExxonMobil wants, every single time. When support for action against the climate crisis rises, he sometimes tweaks his rhetoric ever so slightly. But he never actually does anything to try to solve the problem. To the contrary, he's made it much, much worse."

—*Rolling Stone*, June 12–28, 2007

"A lot of friends of mine in the scientific community are now almost beside themselves in their concern about how the country is failing to act. I frequently hear, 'I don't want to leave my lab, I don't want to stop my research [on global warming, mercury, water pollution, air pollution, the drug-approval process], but I feel like I have to go out on the street corner and start buttonholing people, and I don't think I'm good at that. What can we do?' That's the position they've been put in, because the powers that be don't want to hear the truth. They think they can manufacture their own reality. But in the end, reality has its day. Routinely, the public interest, the health and safety of the public and the integrity of the environment, are all being subordinated to corporate agendas—driven, incidentally by the least responsible companies. There are a lot of great business leaders who understand that this is not working the right way. But [the Bush] administration listens to the least responsible in each industry, and they put their agendas first. And they put the public last."

—*The Stranger* (Seattle), June 1, 2006

"[George Bush] betrayed this country! He played on our fears. He took America on an ill-conceived foreign adventure dangerous to our troops, an adventure preordained and planned before 9/11 ever took place!"

—speech at a rally held by Tennessee Democrats,
February 8, 2004

"[Bush] has exposed Americans abroad and Americans in every U.S. town and city to a greater danger of attack by terrorists because of his arrogance, willfulness, and bungling at stirring up hornets' nests that pose no threat whatsoever to us. And by then insulting the religion and culture and tradition of people in other countries. And by pursuing policies that have resulted in the deaths of thousands of innocent men, women and children, all of it done in our name."

—speech to MoveOn.org, New York City, May 26, 2004

"The Bush administration has fostered false impressions and misled the nation with superficial, emotional and manipulative presentations that are not worthy of American Democracy. They have exploited public fears for partisan political gain and postured themselves as bold defenders of our country while actually weakening not strengthening America. In both cases, they have used unprecedented secrecy and deception in order to avoid accountability to the Congress, the Courts, the press and the people."

—speech to the American Constitution Society,
Washington, D.C., November 9, 2003

"Over the past 18 months, I have delivered a series of speeches addressing different aspects of President Bush's agenda, including his decision to go to war in Iraq under patently false pretenses, his dangerous assault on civil liberties here at home, his outrageously fraudulent economic policy, and his complete failure to protect the global environment. Initially, my purposes were limited in each case to the subject matter of the speech. However, as I tried to interpret what was driving these various policies, certain common features became obvious and a clear pattern emerged: in every instance they have resorted to the language and politics of fear in order to short-circuit debate and drive the public agenda."
—speech at the New School, New York City, February 4, 2004

"The last time we had a president who had the idea that he was above the law was when Richard Nixon told an interviewer, 'When the president does it, that means that it is not illegal. If the president, for example approves something, approves an action because of national security, or, in this case, because of a threat to internal peace and order, of significant order, then the president's decision in this instance is one that enables those who carry it out to carry it out without violating the law.' Fortunately for our country, Nixon was forced to resign as President before he could implement his outlandish interpretation of the Constitution, but not before his defiance of the Congress and the courts created a serious constitutional crisis. In some ways, our current President is actually claiming signif-

icantly more extra-constitutional power, vis-à-vis Congress and the courts, than Nixon did. For example, Nixon never claimed that he could imprison American citizens indefinitely without charging them with a crime and without letting them see a lawyer or notify their families."
—speech to the American Constitution Society, Georgetown University Law Center, Washington D.C, June 24, 2004

"Under our current President Bush, however, the machinery of fear is right out in the open, operating at full throttle."
—speech at the New School, New York City, February 4, 2004

"The [Bush] administration also did not hesitate to use fear of terrorism to launch a broadside attack on measures that have been in place for a generation to prevent a repetition of gross abuses of authority by the FBI and by the intelligence community at the height of the Cold War. I served on the House Select Committee on Intelligence immediately after the period when the revelations of these abuses led to major reforms. Conservatives on that panel resisted those changes tooth and nail. They have long memories, and now these same constraints have been targeted in the Patriot Act and have been sharply diminished or removed."
—speech at the New School, New York City, February 4, 2004

"President Bush has stretched this new practical imperative beyond what is healthy for our democracy. Indeed, one of the ways he has tried to maximize his power within the American system has been by constantly emphasizing his role as Commander-in-Chief, far more than any previous President— assuming it as often and as visibly as he can, and bringing it into the domestic arena and conflating it with his other roles: as head of government and head of state—and especially with his political role as head of the Republican Party. Indeed, the most worrisome new factor, in my view, is the aggressive ideological approach of the current administration, which seems determined to use fear as a political tool to consolidate its power and to escape any accountability for its use."

—speech to the American Constitution Society,
Washington, D.C., November 9, 2003

"Throughout American history, what we now call civil liberties have often been abused and limited during times of war and perceived threats to security. The best known instances include the Alien and Sedition Acts of 1798-1800, the brief suspension of *habeas corpus* during the Civil War, the extreme abuses during World War I and the notorious Red Scare and Palmer Raids immediately after the war, the shameful internment of Japanese-Americans during World War II, and the excesses of the FBI and CIA during the Vietnam War and social turmoil of the late 1960s and early 1970s. But in each of these cases, the nation has recovered its equilibrium when the war ended and absorbed the lessons learned in a recurring cycle of excess and regret. There are reasons for concern this time around that what we are experiencing may no longer be the first half of a recurring cycle, but rather the beginning of something new. For one thing, this war is predicted by the [Bush] administration to 'last for the rest of our lives.' If that is the case, then when—if ever—does this encroachment on our freedoms die a natural death?"

—speech to the American Constitution Society, Washington, D.C., November 9, 2003

"The central elements of President Bush's political, as opposed to religious, belief system are actually plain to see. First, the public interest is a dangerous myth according to Bush's ideology—a fiction created by those hated liberals who use the notion of public interest as an excuse to take away from the wealthy and powerful what they do believe is their due. This is the reason, for example, that President Bush put the former chairman of Enron, Ken Lay, in charge of vetting all of the Bush appointees to the Federal Energy Regulatory Commission. Enron had already helped the Bush team with such favors as ferrying their rent-a-mob to Florida in 2000 to permanently halt the counting of legally cast ballots."

—speech at Georgetown University, Washington, D.C., October 18, 2004

"The Administration has tried to control the flow of information by consistently resorting to the language and politics of fear. Fear drives out reason. Fear suppresses the politics of discourse and opens the door to the politics of destruction. Justice Brandeis once wrote: 'Men feared witches and burnt women.'"
—speech to the American Constitution Society, Washington, D.C., January 16, 2006 (MLK Day)

"The President and I agree on one thing. The threat from terrorism is all too real. There is simply no question that we continue to face new challenges in the wake of the attack on September 11th and that we must be ever-vigilant in protecting our citizens from harm. Where we disagree is on the proposition that we have to break the law or sacrifice our system of government in order to protect Americans from terrorism. When in fact, doing so would make us weaker and more vulnerable. And remember that once violated, the rule of law is itself in danger. Unless stopped, lawlessness grows. The greater the power of the executive grows, the more difficult it becomes for the other branches to perform their constitutional roles. Once that ability is lost, democracy itself is threatened and we become a government of men and not laws."
—speech to the American Constitution Society, Washington, D.C., January 16, 2006 (MLK Day)

"If the President has the inherent authority to eavesdrop on American citizens without a warrant, imprison American citizens on his own declaration, kidnap and torture, then what can't he do? As a result of this unprecedented claim of new unilateral power [by the Bush administration], the Executive branch has now put our constitutional design at grave risk. The stakes for America's democracy are far higher than has been generally recognized. These claims must be rejected and a healthy balance of power restored to our Republic. Otherwise, the fundamental nature of our democracy may well undergo a radical transformation."

—speech to the American Constitution Society,
Washington, D.C., January 16, 2006 (MLK Day)

"Dammit, whatever happened to the concept of accountability for catastrophic failure? This administration has been by far the most incompetent, inept, and with more moral cowardice, and obsequiousness to their wealthy contributors, and obliviousness to the public interest of any administration in modern history, and probably in the entire history of the country!"

—GQ, December 2006

"What did you feel after the invasion of Iraq when you saw American soldiers holding dog leashes attached to helpless prisoners, 99% of whom, by the way, were innocent of any connection to violence against our troops, much less terrorism—innocent prisoners who were being tortured in our name—what did you feel? But draw a line between the emotions that you felt when you absorbed that news, and the emotions that you felt over the last ten days when you saw those corpses in the water [in New Orleans], when you saw people without food, water, medicine—our fellow citizens left helpless. And I want you to draw another line, connecting those responsible for both of those unbelievable tragedies that embarrassed our nation in the eyes of the world."

—speech to the Sierra Summit, San Francisco,
September 9, 2005

"With a year and a half to go in his term and with no consensus in the nation as a whole to support such a proposition [as impeachment], any realistic analysis of that as a policy option would lead one to question the allocation of time and resources. I don't think it would be likely to be successful."

—*NewsHour*, June 7, 2007

"Bush is insulated—his staff smiles a lot and only gives him the news that he wants to hear. Unfortunately, they still have this delusion that they create their own reality."

—*Rolling Stone*, July 13–27, 2006

POLITICS TODAY:
EXPOSING A FLAWED SYSTEM

"Conventional politics is completely broken. Everybody knows it, in both parties. And, you know, those who are candidates obviously are not going to acknowledge that, and they're in it to win, and God bless them, and may the best person win. But winning in a game that rewards as much superficiality and impressionistic manipulation as this current state of politics requires, you know, that is damaging to our country."

—*NewsHour,* June 7, 2007

"The mental muscles of democracy have begun to atrophy."
—from Al Gore's *The Assault on Reason*

"People are fed up. People in both parties are fed up with the way the system is operating. They feel their votes don't count, their opinions don't matter, that their lives aren't understood, that they're not listened to. They have no meaningful way of participating in the system, and too often they're right about all that. We have to change that to the point where people do feel invited back into the conversation of democracy."

—*The New Republic* online, June 13, 2007

"The American people are not well-served by having an end-less [presidential] campaign. We are 500 days away from the next election. So why just sort of close up the field and say, 'Okay, this is it. Place your bets.' I don't have to play that game."

—*CNN Larry King Live*, May 22, 2007

"The solutions to what ails American democracy will take some time and will have to come from a broad engagement by people who do use the new opportunities and tools that are becoming available. Out of that evolutionary process there may emerge opportunities for new kinds of candidates in both parties."

—Politico.com, May 31, 2007

"It is no accident that [an] assault on the integrity of our constitutional design has been fueled by a small group claiming special knowledge of God's will in American politics. They even claim that those of us who disagree with their point of view are waging war against 'people of faith.' How dare they?"
—speech to MoveOn.org, Washington, D.C., April 27, 2005

"The relative role of reason in American political discourse has declined dramatically."

"If either major political party is ever so beguiled by a lust for power that it abandons this unifying principle, then the fabric of our democracy will be torn."

"The Republican Party became merely the name plate for the radical right in this country. The radical right is, in fact, a coalition of those who fear other Americans: as agents of treason; as agents of confiscatory government; as agents of immorality. This fear gives the modern Republican Party its well-noted cohesiveness and its equally well-noted practice of jugular politics. Even in power, the modern Republican Party feels itself to be surrounded by hostility: beginning with government itself, which they present as an enemy."
—speech at the New School, New York City, February 4, 2004

"One reason that the American people are upset about what the Republican Party is doing, is that while they are wasting time on their extremist agenda, they are neglecting issues like the crisis in the cost and availability of health care, the difficulty middle class families are having in making ends meet, etc."
—speech to MoveOn.org, Washington, D.C., April 27, 2005

"I am under no illusion that there is any position that even approaches that of president in terms of an inherent ability to affect the course of events."
—*New York Times*, June 5, 2007

"The survival of freedom depends upon the rule of law."

"Long before our founders met in Philadelphia, their forebears first came to these shores to escape oppression at the hands of despots in the old world who mixed religion with politics and claimed dominion over both their pocketbooks and their souls."
—speech to MoveOn.org, Washington, D.C., April 27, 2005

"The single most surprising new element in America's national conversation is the prominence and intensity of constant fear. Moreover, there is an uncharacteristic and persistent confusion about the sources of that fear; we seem to be having unusual difficult distinguishing between illusory and legitimate ones."
—from Al Gore's *The Assault on Reason*

"In an atmosphere of constant fear, the public is more likely to discard reason and turn to leaders who demonstrate dogmatic faith in ideological viewpoints. These new demagogues don't actually offer greater security from danger, but their simplistic and frequently vitriolic beliefs and statements can provide comfort to a fearful society. Unfortunately, the rise of these leaders serves only to exacerbate the decline of reason and further jeopardize our democracy."
—from Al Gore's *The Assault on Reason*

"Most people of faith I know in both parties have been getting a belly-full of this extremist push to cloak their political agenda in religiosity and mix up their version of religion with their version of right-wing politics and force it on everyone else. They should learn that religious faith is a precious freedom and not a tool to divide and conquer."
—speech to MoveOn.org, Washington, D.C., April 27, 2005

"At least where the presidency is concerned, there is still some symmetry between the skills needed to be elected and the skills needed to govern. After all, the ability of the president to communicate effectively on television is essential. But there is this problem: while a president elected primarily because of an appealing image and personality may be able to communicate effectively, that is no guarantee that he or she can deal with the substance of our government politics or provide a clear, inspiring vision of our national destiny."

—from Al Gore's *Earth in the Balance*

"The second pillar of [the right wing] coalition are social conservatives, many of whom want to roll back most of the progressive social changes of the twentieth century, including many women's rights, social integration, the social safety net, the government social programs of the progressive era, the New Deal, the Great Society, and their coalition includes a number of powerful interest groups like the National Rifle Association, the anti-abortion coalition, and other groups that have agreed to support each other's agendas in order to obtain their own. You could call it the 300 Musketeers, one for all and all for one."

—speech at Georgetown University, Washington, D.C., October 18, 2004

"Yet today's Republicans seem hell-bent on squelching the ability of the minority in this country to express dissent. This is in keeping with other Republican actions to undercut the legislative process. When they decide instead to break the rules and push our democracy into uncharted, uncertain terrain, the results are often not to the liking of the American people. That's what happened when they broke precedents to pass special legislation in the Terri Schiavo case—by playing politics with the Schiavo family tragedy. And, the overwhelming majority of Americans in both political parties told the President and the Congress that they strongly disagreed with that extremist approach."

—speech to MoveOn.org, Washington, D.C., April 27, 2005

"MoveOn.org tried to buy ads last year to express opposition to Bush's Medicare proposal which was then being debated by Congress. They were told 'issue advocacy' was not permissible. Then, one of the networks that had refused the MoveOn ad began running advertisements by the White House in favor of the President's Medicare proposal. So MoveOn complained and the White House ad was temporarily removed. By temporary, I mean it was removed until the White House complained and the network immediately put the ad back on, yet still refused to present the MoveOn ad."

—speech at the American Press Institute, Reston, Virginia, October 5, 2005

"Now the wealthiest and the most powerful completely dominate the conversation. And so, for example, if you take two issues, the need to give affordable health care to 40 million families that don't have it today or the alleged need to permanently eliminate any inheritance tax on the one-tenth of one percent of the billionaires who are the only ones that still are subject to it, why is it that that second issue seems in the public dialogue to be a matter of great urgency and the first one is completely ignored? The reason is those who are affected by the first one have enough money to dominate the conversation. That is dangerous."

—*The Tennessean*, June 2, 2007

"I was elected to the Congress in 1976, served eight years in the house, eight years in the Senate, presided over the Senate for eight years as Vice President. As a young man, I saw the Congress first hand as the son of a Senator. My father was elected to Congress in 1938, ten years before I was born, and left the Senate after I had graduated from college. The Congress we have today is structurally unrecognizable compared to the one in which my father served. It is the pitiful state of our legislative branch which primarily explains the failure of our vaunted checks and balances to prevent the dangerous overreach by the Executive branch now threatening a radical transformation of the American system. The Executive branch, time and again, has co-opted Congress' role, and too often Congress has been a willing accomplice in the surrender of its own power."

—speech to the American Constitution Society, Washington, D.C., January 16, 2006 (MLK Day)

"Our democracy is supposed to operate more often than not according to the rule of reason. A well-informed citizenry, to use the phrase our founders revered, has a conversation according to the best evidence available and tries to make the best decision. But that's not how it works today. That's what's gone wrong."

—Rolling Stone, June 28, 2007

"Unfortunately the virulent faction now committed to changing the basic nature of democracy now wields enough political power within the Republican Party to have a major influence over who secures the Republican nomination for president in the 2008 election. It appears painfully obvious that some of those who have their eyes on that nomination are falling all over themselves to curry favor with this faction."

—speech to MoveOn.org, Washington, D.C., April 27, 2005

"Some of the scandals of Florida four years ago are now being repeated in broad daylight, even as we meet here today. *Harper's* magazine reports in an article published today that tens of thousands of registered voters unjustly denied their right to vote four years ago have still not been allowed back on the rolls."

—speech at Georgetown University,
Washington, D.C., October 18, 2004

"The real reason I wrote [*The Assault on Reason*] is that I've tried for years to tell the story of the climate crisis, and it has taken far too long to get through. When the best evidence is compiled and there's no longer room for dragging out a pointless argument, we're raised as Americans to believe our democracy is going to respond. But it hasn't responded. We're still not doing anything. So I started thinking, 'What's going on here?' In both [the climate crisis and Iraq War], our democracy was pushed around by false impressions and wasn't able to hold its focus. That's the common denominator. Once I'd thought through all of that, I couldn't not write this book."

—*Time*, May 16, 2007

"In the United States today, the politics of reason faces a head wind."

—*Rolling Stone*, June 28, 2007

"This aggressive new strain of right-wing religious zealotry is actually a throwback to the intolerance that led to the creation of America in the first place. James Madison warned us in Federalist #10 that sometimes, 'A religious sect may degenerate into a political faction.'"

—speech to MoveOn.org, Washington, D.C., April 27, 2005

"The essential alchemy of democracy—whereby just power is derived from the consent of the governed—can only occur in a process that is genuinely deliberative."
—speech to MoveOn.org, Washington, D.C., April 27, 2005

"I'm deeply concerned that the role of reason, and facts, and logic in the way we make our decisions in America has been diminished significantly, to the point where we could make a decision to invade a country that didn't attack us, at a time when 70 percent of the American people genuinely had the impression and belief that Saddam Hussein was responsible for the attacks of 9/11. In the same way that the truth about 9/11 was ignored in the rush to war, the truth about the climate crisis has been ignored in the shaping of policies that basically do nothing to stop the most serious crisis our civilization has ever faced."
—*NewsHour*, June 7, 2007

"I am genuinely dismayed and deeply concerned by the recent actions of some Republican leaders to undermine the rule of law by demanding the Senate be stripped of its right to unlimited debate where the confirmation of judges is concerned, and even to engage in outright threats and intimidation against federal judges with whom they philosophically disagree."
—speech to MoveOn.org, Washington, D.C., April 27, 2005

"Sometimes, the political system is like the climate system, in that it's nonlinear. It can seem to change at a snail's pace and then suddenly cross a tipping point beyond which it shifts into a shockingly fast gear. All of a sudden, change that everybody thought was impossible becomes matter of fact. In 1941, it was absurd to think the U.S. could build a thousand airplanes a month to fight the Second World War. By 1943 that was a real small number."

—*Rolling Stone*, July 13–27, 2006

"The $E=mc^2$ of American democracy was John Locke's equation: *All just power derives from the consent of the governed.* It was assumed by our Founders that consent of the governed would be derived through a free and open exchange of ideas in which the merits of proposals and ideas would be tested against the rule of reason, and although it was never a perfect system, and was always mixed with emotion and instinct and passion, nevertheless, reason played the most prominent role. And if that's gone, if reason is taken away, it creates a vacuum that is filled by extreme partisanship, fundamentalism, extreme nationalism, corruption and special interest manipulations, and all of those things are now bedeviling our democracy."

—*The New Republic* online, June 13, 2007

"My book, *The Assault on Reason,* bubbled up because of my growing concern that in order to solve the climate crisis, we are going to have to address the problems in the foundations of our democracy that have kept us from acting on the basis of clear evidence that this crisis is real."

—*CNN Larry King Live,* May 22, 2007

"Our democracy is in danger of being hollowed out."

—from Al Gore's *The Assault on Reason*

"Many Americans now feel that our government is unrespon-sive and that no one in power listens to or cares what they think. They feel disconnected from democracy. They feel that one vote makes no difference, and that they, as individuals, have no practical means of participating in America's self-govern-ment. Unfortunately, they are not entirely wrong."

—from Al Gore's *The Assault on Reason*

"We should have the most important debates [in Congress] in prime time, so that the American people could watch if they choose to. Congress and all parts of the government should be transparent to those citizens who wish to contact them over the Internet and get a minute-by-minute, second-by-second account of what's going on, and give their own opinions during the process."

—*Countdown with Keith Olbermann,* May 29, 2007

"Allowing special interests with the most money to dominate the megaphones in the public square that drowned out the voices of average folks that don't have a lot of money or power is a sure-fire recipe for driving this country's policies over the cliff. We've got to open up the public square so that it's opened again to people who don't have millions of dollars to pay for tickets of admission."

—*The Tennessean,* June 2, 2007

"God does not join political parties."

—*Charlie Rose,* May 25, 2007

"What politics has become requires a level of tolerance for triviality and artifice and nonsense that I find I have in short supply."
—interview with *New York Times* op-ed columnist
Bob Herbert, June 5, 2007

"It wasn't, 'We the conglomerates.' It wasn't, 'We the corporations.' It was, 'We the people.'"
—*Philadelphia Daily News*, October, 21 2005

"And let's make sure that this time every vote is counted. Let's make sure that the Supreme Court does not pick the next president, and that this president is not the one who picks the next Supreme Court."
—address at the 2004 Democratic National Convention

"People don't care that much any more about what's said on the floor of the Senate because the news media doesn't cover it any more. The Senators are often not there, because the system that we have now makes them feel like they have to go out and spend all their time raising money to buy 30-second television commercials, because that's the principal way that political dialogue takes place now."
—*The Daily Show with Jon Stewart,* May 25, 2007

"Once it is widely accepted, cynicism—the stubborn, unwavering disbelief in the possibility of good—can become a malignant habit in democracy. Cynicism is deadly. It bites everything it can reach—like a dog with a foot caught in a trap. And then it devours itself. It drains us of the will to improve; it diminishes our public spirit; it saps our inventiveness; it withers our souls."
—Harvard Commencement Day Address, June 9, 1994

"I really believe that our country would be better off if we had a sharing of power with the legislative branch holding the President accountable, and I'm going to try to help Democrats this fall, but I'm focused on this climate crisis, and I believe it should not be seen as a political issue. I think it is a moral issue, and I want Republicans and conservatives as well as Democrats, liberals, to share the sense of urgency and this moral cause. Our future is at stake."
—CNN *Larry King Live*, June 13, 2006

"The use of the Internet to raise money in small denominations from large numbers of small donors offered a pathway into a different kind of campaign financing. But special interest money is still dominant, and K Street is still dominant. And the explosion of the number of lobbyists in this town just in the last six years is really astonishing. But money now plays a bigger role in the passage of laws and the shaping of policy than it ever has in the worst periods of American history—during the Gilded Age. We really have to address it and correct it. And money is in direct competition with reason."

—*The New Republic* online, June 13, 2007

"Anytime somebody tells you that their vote doesn't count, tell them to come talk to me."

—*Washington Post,* November 17, 2002

U.S. FOREIGN POLICY

"We've over-learned the lessons of Vietnam."

—speaking in 1984

"We must shape the field of history so that it does not lead us inexorably to fields of battle. What is essential is to use military force only in the right way, at the right time, for the right reasons."

—U.S. Military Academy Commencement Address, West Point, May 27, 2000

"I still think Vietnam was a big mistake, but it was the feelings of the ordinary Vietnamese people in the South who were terrified of losing their freedom that had an effect on me. Especially Catholics were terrified of a Communist victory and that sure didn't fit into the cartoon image I had before I went over."

—*New York Times,* July 11, 2000

"If you're a part of something, a war, you want to win it. Not that I had a bayonet in my teeth [in Vietnam], but part of what was screwed up about it was that we weren't trying to win."

—*New York Times,* July 11, 2000

"I have struggled to confront this issue [and] to strike a balance. The risks of war are horrendous. The real costs of war are also horrendous. But what are the costs and risks if the alternative policy does not work? I think they are larger, greater, more costly."

—speaking to reporters after he joined nine other Democrats who broke ranks on a 52-47 Senate vote to authorize the use of force in the 1991 Gulf War

Q: If you had been president, would any of these military interventions not have happened: Lebanon?
A: That was a mistake.
Q: Grenada?
A: I supported that.
Q: Panama?
A: I supported that one.
Q: Persian Gulf?
A: Yes, I voted for it, supported it.

Q: Somalia?
A: That was ill considered. I did support it at the time. In retrospect the lessons there are ones that we should take very seriously.
Q: Bosnia.
A: Oh, yes.
Q: Haiti?
A: Yes.
Q: And then Kosovo.
A: Yes.

—from presidential debate in Winston-Salem,
North Carolina, October, 11, 2000

"I am very troubled by [Putin's] apparent backtracking on press freedom for Russia in the post-communist era. I am very troubled obviously by their conduct in Chechnya. We have to put first things first, and recognize that the U.S. has an abiding interest in continuing to manage the nuclear threat, and we should not ever forget that Russia has thousands of nuclear warheads and the delivery systems capable of targeting them on the U.S."

—speaking to reporters in Ohio, October 4, 2000

"Let's take the case of Bosnia. Here we had the most violent and bloody war in Europe since World War II, in an area of Europe that spawned the conflicts that became World War I. A growing instability that threatened to touch off a chain reaction that would spill over border after border and lead to a much wider conflict and disorder. And at the heart of the festering wound was what they called, in the repugnant phrase they coined, ethnic cleansing. It was a hard decision for the United States to get involved. But it was in my view, clearly, the right decision."

—speaking to reporters in Ohio, October 4, 2000

"'Ethnic cleansing' is a phrase intended to mask the stench of its true meaning: the combination of mass murder and mass expulsion. 'Ethnic cleansing' means that a dictator can simply throw away the people he does not need—like so much dirt and disease. It dehumanizes along ethnic lines, so that murder and displacement become scientific, antiseptic, something other than atrocity. So I say to Milosevic: we are not fooled by your hateful rhetoric. We see through your veil of evil—and we will stop it."

—speech on fiftieth anniversary of NATO, Ellis Island, New York, April 21, 1999

"If what America represents to the world is leadership in a commonwealth of equals, then our friends are legion. If what we represent to the world is empire, then it is our enemies who will be legion."

—speech at the Commonwealth Club, San Francisco,
September 23, 2002

"All developed countries—whether in Asia, Europe, or the Americas—must play a role, and keep tearing down trade barriers. In the end, in this global economy, protectionism will only protect us from prosperity itself. And as we open the doors to global trade wider than ever before, let us build a trading system that lifts the fortunes of more and more people. Let us include strong protections for workers, for health and safety, for a clean environment. For at its heart, global commerce is about strengthening our shared global values. It is about building stronger families and stronger communities, through strong and steady growth around the world. That is why the future of free and robust global markets depends so strongly on a third challenge—one that surpasses all the others, even as it supports all the others. It is democracy, and the growth of self-government around the world."

—speech at APEC Business Summit, Kuala Lumpur,
November 16, 1998

"I think that we need to demand the respect for human rights and religious freedom. But bringing China into the community of nations, fostering peace between China and Taiwan and engaging them in a way that furthers our values, I think that's in our interest."

—Democratic presidential primary debate in Durham, New Hampshire, January 5, 2000

"The last four presidents in both political parties have purposely refrained from spelling out the details of what would trigger a direct military action by the U.S. in the Taiwan Straits. That ambiguity is not due to a failure to think it through; it is due to a considered judgment that we do not want to give the hotheads on either side of the Taiwan Straits an ability to drive circumstances toward American involvement for their own purposes."

—Democratic presidential primary debate in Los Angeles, California, March 1, 2000

"The future of the world depends, more than many realize, on the healing of Africa's place in the world. It's the big missing piece. Just as the emergence of Latin America over the last few decades resulted in the fastest-growing markets for the U.S. economy, so the emergence of Africa in the next decade can lift the world economy to new heights. The potential is vast, but the problems are daunting. We have to avoid what is called 'Afro-pessimism.' Because for every horror story—and there are lots of them—there are less prominent success stories."

—*Rolling Stone,* November 9, 2000

"The practicalities of modern warfare which necessarily increase the war powers of the President at the expense of Congress do not render moot the concerns our founders had so long ago that the making of war by the president—when added to his other powers—carries with it the potential for unbalancing the careful design of our constitution, and in the process, threatening our liberty. They were greatly influenced— far more than we can imagine—by a careful reading of the history and human dramas surrounding the democracies of ancient Greece and the Roman republic. They knew, for example, that democracy disappeared in Rome when Caesar crossed the Rubicon in violation of the Senate's long prohibition against a returning general entering the city while still in command of military forces. Though the Senate lingered in form and was humored for decades, when Caesar impoliticly combined his military commander role with his chief executive role, the Senate—and with it the Republic—withered away. And then for all intents and purposes, the great dream of democracy disappeared from the face of the Earth for seventeen centuries, until its rebirth in our land."

—American Constitution Society speech, Georgetown University Law Center, Washington, D.C., June 24, 2004

"I have always believed that America needs a strong Europe—
as an economic partner, helping to shoulder the burdens of
global economic leadership in the global economy, and also as
a security partner to work with us in defending freedom and
democracy against rogue states and dictators in this post-Cold
War world. That is why my approach toward Europe has always
been one of engagement—through open and fair trading rela-
tionships, and through NATO and other security alliances that
defend our common values."

—Gore 2000 campaign web page, April 1999

Q: Your administration did little to evict Osama bin Laden
from Afghanistan after the terrorist attacks in the embassies in
Kenya and Tanzania. Why?

A: We took many steps to try to eliminate him and his terrorist network. The support here at home, much less overseas,
for a land invasion of Afghanistan by the armies of the United
States was not present in any way prior to the attack on
September 11. We did attack with our military forces from the
air. We did use many of the assets that we have available to us,
covert as well as overt, in an effort to dismantle his network.

—remarks following speech at the Commonwealth Club,
San Francisco, September 23, 2002

"Nuclear unilateralism will hinder, rather than help, arms control."
—*New York Times,* May 28, 2000

"One final word on this proposed doctrine of preemption; this goes far beyond the situation in Iraq. It would affect the basic relationship between the United States and the rest of the world community. Article 51 of the United Nations charter approved here recognizes the right of any nation to defend itself, including the right to take preemptive actions in order to deal with imminent threats. President Bush now asserts that we will take preemptive action even if the threat we perceive is not imminent. If other nations assert that same right, then the rule of law will quickly be replaced by the reign of fear."
—speech at the Commonwealth Club, San Francisco,
September 23, 2002

"I believe that we can effectively defend ourselves abroad and at home without dimming our core principles. Indeed, I believe that our success in defending ourselves depends precisely on not giving up what we stand for. We should have as our top priority preserving what America represents and stands for in the world and winning the war against terrorism first."
—speech at the Commonwealth Club, San Francisco,
September 23, 2002

THE PROMISE OF AMERICA AND
THE CHALLENGE OF DEMOCRACY

"I feel passionately about the need to fix the cracks in the foundation of American democracy. We made this mistake in Iraq and we're making this even worse mistake on the climate crisis because facts and logic and reason are not playing the role they should."

—CNN Larry King Live, July 5, 2007

"I'm an American citizen. I'm going to continue speaking out on my views forcefully and as best I can."

—Countdown with Keith Olbermann, May 29, 2007

"While we yet hold and do not yield our opposing beliefs, there is a higher duty than the one we owe to political party. This is America and we put country before party."

—televised presidential concession speech, December 13, 2000

"Sometimes people who have great dreams, as young people do, are apt to stay at arm's length from the political process because they think if they invest their hopes, they're going to be disappointed. But thank goodness we've always had enough people who have been willing to push past the fear of a broken heart and become deeply involved in forming a more perfect union."
—presidential debate in St Louis, October 17, 2000

"There is good and evil in every person. And what makes the United States special in the history of nations is our commitment to the rule of law and our carefully constructed system of checks and balances. Our natural distrust of concentrated power and our devotion to openness and democracy are what have led us as a people to consistently choose good over evil in our collective aspirations more than the people of any other nation."
—speech to MoveOn.org, New York City, May 26, 2004

"So, it is not as a Democrat but as an American, that I appeal today to the leadership of the majority in the Senate to halt their efforts to break the Senate's rules and instead protect a meaningful role in the confirmation of judges and justices for Senators of both parties. Remember that you will not always be in the majority, but much more importantly, remember what is best for our country regardless of which party is temporarily in power. Many of us know what it feels like to be disappointed with decisions made by the courts. But instead of attacking the judges with whose opinions we disagree, we live by the rule of law and maintain respect for the courts."

—speech to MoveOn.org, Washington, D.C., April 27, 2005

"Democracy is a conversation. The First Amendment's guarantees of freedom of speech, freedom of the press, freedom to petition the government, freedom of assembly, were all aimed at protecting the freedom and integrity of that conversation which our founders felt was at the heart of representative democracy."

—*The New Republic* online, June 13, 2007

"It is time now for us to recover our moral health in America and stand again to rise for freedom, demand accountability for poor decisions, missed judgments, lack of planning, lack of preparation, and willful denial of the obvious truth about serious and imminent threats that are facing the American people."

—speech at the Sierra Summit, San Francisco,
September 9, 2005

"The dance of democracy is always between whoever is leading the country and what James Madison described as a well-informed citizenry. And renewing that political will and informing the people of this country about the reality of our circumstances, that's what I'm focused on."

—CNN *Larry King Live,* June 13, 2006

"[The Internet] *is* the single greatest source of hope that we will be able to fix what ails the conversation of democracy. The Internet has low entry barriers for individuals, who are then able to join the conversation. If the Internet had been as strong six years ago as it is now, maybe, maybe there would've been a lot more attention paid to the real facts, and we would not have had our troops stuck over there in the middle of a civil war."

—*The Daily Show with Jon Stewart,* May 25, 2007

"The civil rights movement took off in the United States only when it was lifted out of the political framework and placed in a spiritual framework. Young people asked their parents, 'You tell me to choose right over wrong, so explain to me why this guy Bull Connor is acceptable.' When the adults couldn't answer, that's when the laws changed. Young people are now asking their parents and grandparents, 'Please explain to me why what's going on with global warming isn't insane.' A lot of adults can't answer. The revolution is beginning."

—*Rolling Stone,* June 12–28, 2007

"The root word for democracy—*demos*—meant the masses of common people, who were an object of fear in the minds of many of our country's founders. What they wanted was an orderly society in which property would be safe from arbitrary confiscation (remember the Revolutionary War was in significant measure about taxation). What they believed was that a too pure democracy would expose that society to the ungoverned passions of what today we call 'the street': of people with little to lose, whose angers could be all too easily aroused by demagogues (note the root, again) and turned against those with wealth. So the Constitution of which we are so proud is really an effort—based at least as much on fear as on hope—to compromise and balance out the conflicting agendas of two kinds of Americans: those who already have achieved material success, and those who aspire to it: those who are happy with the status quo, and those who can only accept the status quo if it is the jumping off place to something better for themselves. That tension can never be fully resolved, and it is perfectly clear at the present moment in the profoundly differing agendas of our two major parties."

—speech at the New School, New York City,
February 4, 2004

"The American democratic system was an early political version of Napster. [It] made it possible for the average citizen to participate in the decision-making of this nation."

—*Red Herring*, October 30, 2000

"In spite of the cultural soul sickness we've confronted recently, there is a goodness in Americans that, when mobilized, is more than a match for it This hunger for goodness manifests itself in a newly vigorous grassroots movement tied to non-profit institutions, many of them faith-based and values-based organizations. People are engaged in the deeply American act of not waiting for government to deal with the problems on their own doorsteps. Instead, they are casting a vote for their own wise hearts and strong hands to take care of their own."

—speech in Atlanta, Georgia, May 24, 1999

"Vigilant adherence to the rule of law actually strengthens our democracy, of course, and strengthens America."
—speech to the American Constitution Society, Washington, D.C., January 16, 2006 (MLK Day)

"Dashed hopes poison our political will just as surely as chemical waste can poison drinking water aquifers deep in the ground."
—Harvard Commencement Day Address, June 9, 1994

"A commitment to openness, truthfulness, and accountability helps our country avoid many serious mistakes, that we would otherwise make."
—speech to the American Constitution Society, Washington, D.C., January 16, 2006 (MLK Day)

"Our mission has always been to prove that religious, political, and economic liberty are the natural birthright of all men and women, and that freedom unlocks a higher fraction of the human potential than any other way of organizing human society. America has a [second] mission to prove to the world that people of different racial and ethnic backgrounds, of all

faiths and creeds, can not only work and live together, but can enrich and ennoble both themselves and our common purpose."
—speech on fiftieth anniversary of NATO, Ellis Island, New York, April 21, 1999

"There is a difference between using the right language, and seeing the right connections between new policies and progress—between talking about compassion, and actually putting your highest ideals into practice. America needs something better than compassionate conservatism—we need an approach that will take this country forward, not backward; and not only forward, but also upward. The Republicans seem always to be pulled backward before they can translate their rhetoric into policies their party can actually support."
—1998 Democratic Leadership Council Annual Conference, Washington, D.C., December 2, 1998

"I see a day—and I tell you that day is coming—when we will achieve, in ways both practical and bold, health coverage for every child in America, and then health coverage for every American."
—speech in Atlanta, Georgia, January 17, 2000 (MLK Day)

"We often tend to romanticize the past, of course, and there never was a golden age when reason resigned supreme, banishing falsehood and demagoguery from the deliberations of American self-government. But for all of America's shortcomings in the past, we did usually strive to honor truth and reason."

—from Al Gore's *The Assault on Reason*

"Today, 32 years after we lost him, America still needs the soaring dream of Martin Luther King. We need your prophetic voice—and we hear it now, even from the grave, the words and the ideals that will never die. We need those thundering words; we need those righteous ideals. As we have been reminded, 'We shall overcome' must be more than a memory from the past. It must be a resolve to find the true America at last."

—speech in Atlanta, Georgia, January 17, 2000 (MLK Day)

"Don't tell me we have a color-blind society. I have a different view: I believe that America still needs affirmative action."

—speech at NAACP Annual Convention, July 16, 1998

"America's principal mission in human history has always been to advance the cause of liberty and to prove that religious, political, and economic freedom unlock a higher fraction of the human potential than any other way of organizing human society."
—New York University Commencement Address,
New York City, May 14, 1998

"In spite of serious challenges we believe America must address on behalf of families, we are optimistic because we believe that our nation is strong and creative and bighearted enough to rise to meet these challenges. For us, as for most Americans, family is our bedrock. Now, because of the profound transformation of American families over the last forty years, it is time to examine all of the changes that have taken place. It is time to boldly address the urgent need to provide every appropriate support to every kind of family—and so make it possible for all of us to discover the lasting joy and deep sense of connection by those who are joined at the heart."
—from Al and Tipper Gore's *Joined at the Heart*

"Just as a single tumbling rock can trigger a massive landslide, America has sometimes experienced sudden avalanches of political change that had their beginnings with what first seemed like small changes. Two weeks ago, Democrats and Republicans joined together in our largest state, California, to pass legally binding sharp reductions in CO_2 emissions. Two hundred and ninety-five American cities have now independently 'ratified' and embraced CO_2 reductions called for in the Kyoto Treaty. Eighty-five conservative evangelical ministers publicly broke with the Bush-Cheney administration to call for bold action to solve the climate crisis."

—speech at New York University School of Law,
New York City, September 18, 2006

"Individual Americans of all ages are becoming a part of a movement, asking what they can do as individuals and what they can do as consumers and as citizens and voters. Many individuals and businesses have decided to take an approach known as 'zero carbon.' They are reducing their CO_2 as much as possible and then offsetting the rest with reductions elsewhere including by the planting of trees. At least one entire community—Ballard, a city of 18,000 people in Washington State—is embarking on a goal of making the entire community zero carbon."

—speech at New York University School of Law,
New York City, September 18, 2006

Q: Should English be made the country's official language?
A: I believe that all of our people should have the opportunity to learn English, so that they can succeed and reach their fullest potential. However, I oppose "English only" proposals. Everyone knows that English is the language of the United States. "English only" laws only seek to divide our nation, which has a long history of immigration by people who speak many languages.
—Associated Press, November 1, 2000

"To those who say this problem [global warming] is too difficult, I say that we have accepted and met such challenges in the past. We declared our liberty, and then won it. We designed a country that respected and safeguarded the freedom of individuals. We abolished slavery. We gave women the right to vote. We took on Jim Crow and segregation. We cured fearsome diseases, landed on the moon, won two wars simultaneously—in the Pacific and in Europe. We brought down communism, we defeated apartheid."
—Al Gore, "The Time to Act is Now," *Rolling Stone,*
November 3, 2005

"Democracy stands or falls on a mutual trust—government's trust of the people and the people's trust of the governments they elect. And yet at the same time democratic culture and politics have always existed in a strange blend of credulity and skepticism. Democracy did not mean unity in the body politic. People do have reasonable differences. Human ignorance, pride, and selfishness would always be with us, prompting inevitable divisions and conflicting ambitions."

—Harvard Commencement Day Address, June 9, 1994

"The truth is that American democracy is now in danger—not from any one set of ideas, but from the unprecedented changes in the environment within which ideas either live and spread, or wither and die. I do not mean the physical environment. I mean what is called the public sphere, or the marketplace of ideas."

—from Al Gore's *The Assault on Reason*

"My way of understanding [of race relations] has come in large measure from Reinhold Niebuhr's work, and I'm not qualified to paraphrase it, but if I tried I would say it this way: Each of us has an inherent capacity for both good and evil. And if you prefer nonreligious language you could say that the lingering presence of nature red in tooth and claw that we carry with us from our evolutionary development gives us the capacity to strike out violently when we encounter a fearful difference—when we encounter a difference that inspires fear. Groups protect one another. Survival in the ancient past presumably depended on that ready impulse. But our spiritual nature—or, to describe it again in parallel terms, our evolutionary development—has also given us a much richer heritage with which we can overcome the impulse to evil, or violence, triggered by fear of difference."

—*New Yorker,* July 31, 2000

"When we Americans first began, our biggest danger was clearly in view: we knew from the bitter experience with King George III that the most serious threat to democracy is usually the accumulation of too much power in the hands of an Executive, whether he be a King or a president. Our ingrained American distrust of concentrated power has very little to do with the character or persona of the individual who wields that power. It is the power itself that must be constrained, checked, dispersed and carefully balanced, in order to ensure the survival of freedom. In addition, our founders taught us that public fear is the most dangerous enemy of democracy because under the right circumstances it can trigger the temptation of those who govern themselves to surrender that power to someone who promises strength and offers safety, security, and freedom from fear."

—American Constitution Society speech, Georgetown University Law Center, Washington, D. C., June 24, 2004

"The last and best description of America's meaning in the world is still the definitive formulation of Lincoln's annual message to Congress on December 1, 1862: 'The occasion is piled high with difficulty, and we must rise—with the occasion. As our case is new, so we must think anew, and act anew. We must disenthrall ourselves, and then we shall save our country. Fellow citizens, we cannot escape history . . . the fiery trial through which we pass will light us down in honor or dishonor to the latest generation . . . We shall nobly save, or meanly lose the last best hope of earth . . . The way is plain, peaceful, generous, just—a way which, if followed, the world will forever applaud, and God must forever bless.'"

—speech to MoveOn.org, New York City, May 26, 2004

"When the American people are treated as objects for just herding in one direction or another, that's insulting to the integrity of our democracy."

—*Countdown with Keith Olbermann,* May 29, 2007

"When America was founded, our founders said, 'We are not going to pretend that whoever is elected to office has been ordained by the Almighty to be the decision maker. The person who is elected is elected by us, the people of this country.' The divine right of kings was rejected by the founders of the United States. But this has been twisted around in recent times by some people who want to convey the impression that God has a particular political ideology and that those who disagree with a right-wing approach are against God. That is completely contrary to the spirit of America."

—CNN *Larry King Live,* May 22, 2007

Q: How can government reconnect with youth?
A: By just shooting straight—and really trusting people with the unvarnished truth, even if it's hard to hear.

—*Rolling Stone,* November 9, 2000

"We choose our Americas. From today, we can choose an America in the year 2100 that is stable, prosperous, equitable, and at peace, because we will have moved to the highest ground from which to govern. Or we can choose an America in 2100 that is still plagued by false divisions, conflicts, and instabilities that should be relegated to the attic of the past. Let us choose the future that is built on the insight of our mutuality: mutual respect, mutual responsibility, mutual civility, and, in regard to the weakest among us, mutual kindness and care."
—speech at 1998 Democratic Leadership Council Annual Conference, Washington D.C., December 2, 1998

"I have worked on environmental causes for more that two decades now. But in all my years of work on this issue, I have never seen a more hopeful sight that the crowd that is gathered here today. Standing with us are captains of industry; labor leaders and working men and women; Teamsters and auto workers; lifelong environmentalists. Ten years ago, if you'd told me you were assembling this crowd, I'd have thought it was an episode of *Crossfire*. We've come a long way. Today, we're not shouting at one another—we're standing shoulder to shoulder, working together, meeting our responsibility, doing the right thing."
—speech on Earth Day 2000

"America deserves livable communities, comfortable suburbs, vibrant cities, and green spaces all around and in between: not the dumpy trash-strewn cesspools America has devolved into during the last 75 years."
—speech to the American Institute of Architects, May 5, 2007

"I'm trying to say to you, be a part of the change. No one else is going to do it. The politicians are paralyzed. The people have to do it for themselves! Our democracy hasn't been working very well—that's my opinion. We've made a bunch of serious policy mistakes. But it's way too simple and way too partisan to blame the Bush-Cheney Administration. We've got checks and balances, an independent judiciary, a free press, a Congress— have they all failed us? Have we failed ourselves?"
—speaking at University of Buffalo, *Time,* May 16, 2007

"In the aftermath of Hurricane Katrina, there was—at least for a short time—a quality of vividness and clarity of focus in our public discourse that reminded some Americans—including some journalists—that vividness and clarity used to be more common in the way we talk with one another about the problems and choices that we face. But then, like a passing summer storm, the moment faded."
—speech at the American Press Institute, Reston, Virginia, October 5, 2005

"The vitality of our democracy will be re-established by the people."

—speech to the American Constitution Society,
Washington, D.C., January 16, 2006 (MLK Day)

"We need to breathe life back into American democracy. I think I'm making a contribution by speaking my heart as clearly and as boldly as I know how."

—*New York*, May 22, 2006

RUNNING FOR PRESIDENT AGAIN

"I do not expect to ever be a candidate again. If I did expect to be a candidate again, I would probably not feel the same freedom to let it rip in these speeches the way I am. And I enjoy that. It feels liberating to me."

—*New Yorker*, September 13, 2004

"I'm just a recovering politician."

—2006

"I don't want to be responsible for anyone feeling that I'm inching toward running again when I'm not. You won't find a single person in Iowa, New Hampshire, or anywhere who has had the slightest signal that originated with me or anyone speaking for me."

—*New York*, May 22, 2006

Q: Is there any chance that you would run for the presidency again?

A: I don't see any chance. I'm not thinking about that, not planning it, don't expect it. I have said that when pressed on this question as I'm sure you're about to press me, that I haven't reached a point in my life where I'm willing to say never again. But that is more a function of internal gear-shifting, not an effort to be coy and keep the door open to it.

—*Fresh Air with Terry Gross*, NPR,
May 30, 2006

"I will continue to play a role as a citizen, not only on global warming but also on eavesdropping and torture and civil liberties and the other vital issues of the day. I've got a full plate right now. Being a candidate for president again is not part of my plan for the next several years. If I can just figure out a way to appear in the pages of *Rolling Stone* every several months, that will be fulfillment enough."

—*Rolling Stone*, July 13–27, 2006

"Even though I honestly had not planned on doing this, I guess with a billion people watching, it's as good a time as any. So, my fellow Americans, I'm going to take this opportunity right here and now to formally announce . . ."

—pretending to declare that he's running for president before being drowned out by the orchestra during his Academy Awards acceptance speech for best documentary, February 27, 2007

"Having spent 30 years as part of the political dialogue, I don't know why a 600-day campaign is taken as a given. I don't have to play that game."

—*New York Times,* May 20, 2007

"I am not thinking about being a candidate. I have no plans to be a candidate. But, yes, it's true, I have not made a so-called Sherman statement and ruled it out for all time. I see no reason or necessity to do that."

—*CNN Larry King Live,* May 22, 2007

"I don't think that I have to apologize for spending my time on [the climate crisis] rather than getting into this political process. Maybe at some point in the future I will have some interest in doing that again, but I don't feel that right now."

—Charlie Rose, May 25, 2007

"A couple of my friends have said over the last year, 'Al, why don't you take a break and run for president?'"

—The Tennessean, June 2, 2007

"I have no plans to be a candidate for president again. I'm 58 years old. That's the new 57."

—This Week with George Stephanopoulos, June 4, 2006

"I respect the political process with all its flaws, and I am under no illusions that the presidency is not the most important position with the most ability to influence the course of events, but I've run twice and I don't think that my aptitude for politics is necessarily matched to the kind of politics that the system calls for in this day and time. Maybe that will change. Maybe the transformation of this conversation of democracy with more influence for reason and less for image and spin will emerge. but I'm grateful for those who have a good opinion of me, to the point where they think I ought to run again, but I am not convinced myself that's the best way for me to serve."

—*The Tennessean,* June 2, 2007

"The kinds of skills that are rewarded in this new communications environment include some that I don't think I have in abundance—a tolerance for artifice and repetition, an appreciation for clever manipulative strategies."

—*The Guardian* (UK), June 2, 2007

"Tipper leaves it up to me. She is supportive of whatever decision I make."

—*The Tennessean,* June 2, 2007

"I'm uncomfortable speaking as a [presidential] candidate. I don't hold myself out as an authority or a source of any expertise on campaigns. I'm not trying to be falsely modest. I mean I had some successes in electoral politics. [But] if I were a candidate, I would seek to engage people in a robust exchange of ideas."
—*The New Republic* online, June 13, 2007

"I've kind of fallen out of love with politics."
—2007

MISCELLANY

"After flying on Air Force Two for eight years, I have to take off my shoes to get on an airplane."

"Airplane travel is nature's way of making you look like your passport photo."

"They say a lot of comedy is born of pain. My sense of humor always benefits from low expectations."

—*Der Spiegel* (Germany), July 21, 2006

"Doesn't it feel like you woke up one day and found yourself in an alternative reality?"

—at New York City bookstore signing, May 27, 2007

Q: What [is] your favorite Beatles record?
A: *Rubber Soul.*

—*Rolling Stone,* November 9, 2000

"There probably was more than one person, Lee Harvey Oswald, involved [in killing John F. Kennedy]. I believe that. I think most Americans believe that."

—Reuters, July 20, 1992

"I'd just arrived in Vienna on September 11 and when the planes hit the towers, I knew right away it was bin Laden."

—*New York,* May 22, 2006

"When you have the facts on your side, argue the facts. When you have the law on your side, argue the law. When you have neither, holler."

"Tipper and I got a Lexus hybrid. And we have a couple of Priuses in the family with our children."

"This whole notion that I have a tendency to exaggerate or embellish is absolutely ridiculous. In fact, if you look at the movie *Love Story*, you will notice that the Ryan O'Neil character, Oliver Barrett IV, who was based solely on me, never exaggerates even once during the movie. Now, I remember when Erich Segal was writing *Love Story*. He told me, 'Al, I want the main character in *Love Story* to exude the quality that I think of when I think of you, which is that you never exaggerate.' I know some people are going to keep accusing me of exaggeration, so let me be clear. Those people seek nothing less than the complete destruction of the American way of life. It's absolutely clear. I never exaggerate. You can ask Tipper or any one of our eleven daughters."

—speech at the Al Smith Dinner in New York City, October 19, 2000

"Whatever tensions there were [with Bill Clinton] matched the friendship and camaraderie and common purposes. We've just been through too much together. We have a bond that'll never be shaken. We'll never be eclipsed by any disagreement, we just won't be. It's not a brother-to-brother relationship, but it's in that family."

—*New York*, May 22, 2006

"I will say that all the Democrats who supported the [Iraq] war made a mistake, in my opinion. But I'm not going to single [Hillary Clinton] out."

—*New York*, May 22, 2006

"Tipper keeps my shoes nailed to the floor so that I don't lose touch with gravity."

—*Rolling Stone,* November 9, 2000

"Love is such a complicated force, I don't have the words to speak intelligently about it. I don't even want to try to universalize what feels true to me, because everybody's different. And you know, Tipper has a graduate degree in psychology, and she has had a fairly intensive psychiatric practice for 40 years—with one patient. I'm seriously not joking when I say the secret is mostly her. She's just an amazing partner in life."

—*GQ*, December 2006

Q: Is there a burden to being so smart?
A: That's the exact converse of, 'When did you stop beating your wife?' There's no way to answer a question like that without seeming pompous and conceited. I have a battery-powered hubris alarm on my belt. And it's set on vibrate, and it's going crazy.

—*GQ*, December 2006

"I actually don't think I'm particularly good at politics. Well, you know, it dawned on me late in life. I'm just now fighting through the denial."

—*Charlie Rose*, May 25, 2007

"I'm just so filled with enthusiasm and energy, I'm not letting you ask questions."

—to an Associated Press reporter, en route to Live Earth concert at Giants stadium in New Jersey, July 7, 2007

NOTES AND ACKNOWLEDGMENTS

Every reasonable attempt has been made to provide original source material for all Al Gore quotes. Exceptions might include quotes that he often likes to use. Probably the quote with most mileage is his standard warm-up line to audiences: "Hi, I'm Al Gore and I used to be the next president of the United States." It never fails to elicit a good chuckle from listeners.

I need to extend kudos to the Skyhorse Publishing crew for getting this book out in breakneck speed. The entire project was completed in only a matter of several weeks. The idea for this book came from Herman Graf, former publisher of Carroll & Graf, and currently a consultant for Skyhorse Publishing. In turn, Skyhorse publisher Tony Lyons contacted me. Special appreciation also goes to Skyhorse Associate Publisher Bill Wolfsthal for his valuable assistance and ensuring this book took flight.

And finally, I would like to convey my gratitude to Al Gore whose big brain I crawled inside for a brief spell. I wish I could have stayed longer. Personally, I believe that the 2000 election was stolen, and the wrong man got the job. Some blame for

Gore's defeat can be attributed to those vexing *butterfly ballots* which affected voting in southern Florida. A fair electoral system would have mandated a complete statewide recount, something the Supreme Court wrongly dismissed. And so, all that has happened since then is straight out of chaos theory: the slight turbulence created by a *butterfly* flapping its wings can set into motion atmospheric disturbance that results in a hurricane on the other side of the planet.

—BILL KATOVSKY

Bill Katovsky is the author of *Patriots Act: Voices of Dissent and the Risk of Speaking Out* and co-author of *Embedded: The Media at War in Iraq*, which won Harvard's Goldsmith Book Prize.